FROM THE BOOKS OF

Ben Dudley

NINA

NINA

by

Nina van Pallandt

WALKER AND COMPANY
New York

Acknowledgments

My thanks and gratitude to:

Linda Myers, who lovingly worked with me on this book and became my friend;

Don and Gitta Honeyman, my old friends, for help, advice and encouragement;

Heather Mizen, who tapped her fingers off;

Els Teunissen, for keeping my paper-strewn household together.

First published in the United States of America in 1973 by the Walker Publishing Company, Inc.

Published simultaneously in Canada by Fitzhenry & Whiteside, Limited, Toronto.

ISBN: 0-8027-0399-2

Library of Congress Catalog Card Number: 72-83757

Printed in the United States of America.

Book designed by James E. Barry

For my mother
Frederik
Nicolas, Kirsa, Ana Maria

Walk among the tacit trees
Sail across the placid seas
All I see is imperfection
Mirrored in my own reflection
Die and feel the resurrection
Fill me, show me, help me, guide me
For I long for the completion
Of my dreams without cohesion.
Million billion stars and light years,
Am I but a spark of nightfears
Searching for a single reason
Being reborn with each season?
Am I? is it all illusion
Striving, is it past confusion?
Earthlives flowing in profusion
Heart, let love be my conclusion.

——N.v.P.

For "Mommie," my mother-in-law, who died in June, 1972.

Contents

St. Regis

I was famous but felt like a freak, and was damn well going to show them I wasn't. No one in America knew me, save for being "The Danish singer in the Hughes affair." While in New York in February for the grand jury hearings, there'd been dozens of offers for cabarets and television and I don't know what else.

Then when Frank Banks, manager of the St. Regis, suggested an engagement at the hotel's "Maisonette," a small elegant room like the ones I'd been used to working in in Europe, my manager, John Marshall, saw a way of turning the negative into the positive. It would be a three-week engagement, two shows a night, to begin April 3.

On a short holiday home in London after the contract signing, John and I talked it over and agreed, since this would be my debut in the States, to prepare the act there and use only American talent. By February 27 we were flying back to the St. Regis, which was to be our home for the next two months, and home Suite 1003 really became.

John engaged Walter Levinski, with whom I'd worked on my first "Dick Cavett Show" appearance two weeks before, to do the music, and asked Donald Brooks to design my costumes. Walt suggested Derek Smith of the "Johnny Carson

9

Show" as my pianist—how lucky that he was available. We were looking for an acoustic guitar player when inspiration struck me: an old harpist friend of mine, Jack Melady, had called after finding *Life* with my picture on it on his doorstep one morning. In my act, I always do a medley of folk songs with a guitar. Why not do it this time with a harp, an instrument I love just as much? Jack agreed, and during the next three weeks we rehearsed together, dug up old songs and sang and played for our own pleasure.

Every day, I went to Nola's Rehearsal Studios on 57th Street for a couple of hours, partly to work out the arrangements created by Walt and Derek, partly to do voice exercises and have a bit of peace and quiet from the press-besieged madhouse the St. Regis was already becoming. One day at Nola's, there was an audition for a Broadway show going on in the next room. The corridor was lined with young hopefuls and, in my blue jeans, scarf and dark glasses, I guess I passed for one of them. The door suddenly opened and a bearded young chap, clipboard in hand, came rushing out, turned to me and barked, "What's your name and what've you done?" I told him I was just waiting for the room next door, but for one instant, I felt a great longing to be part of that camaraderie in the corridor. I suddenly felt very alone.

Several times a week, I went to Manka Stark's studios for fittings. She is Donald Brooks's head seamstress who fitted and made the individual costumes in her atelier, each fitting carefully scrutinized by Donald himself. I loved to listen to Manka and her assistant nattering away in Polish as they snipped, cut, ripped, and pinned until I most resembled a rag doll. That state, needless to say, was temporary, the results well worth the endless hours of playing mannequin.

John was busy preparing the opening with Frank Banks. Once the date had been announced, the enormous interest and curiosity generated brought countless reservations, especially from the press for opening night. I appeared on the "Mike Douglas," "Johnny Carson" and "David Frost" shows while John was juggling the dozens of interview requests from newspapers, magazines, fashion columnists, overseas networks and wire services, and sorting out the ever-increasing stream of offers of every kind.

In the midst of it all, my housekeeper/nanny in London had left overnight because of a death in the family, and I flew home to see the children and clean the flat. In response to an S.O.S. from Frederik, my husband from whom I am separated, our old Scottish nanny came back temporarily, tailoring her office job to the children's schedules, bless her soul. At the same time, my mother and her longtime housekeeper, Saasi, were mopping up two feet of water from a burst boiler in her Copenhagen flat. It was a rough spring for everyone. Sassi's been with the family for twenty years, almost more "family" than we are. There isn't anything she can't do or won't do for any of us, and many's the time she's been the emergency helping hand in my far-flung households. The children worship her, and their conversations in half-Danish, half-English are hilarious. As soon as she'd wrung out the mops in Copenhagen, she pitched in here, too, taking over my household and the children until I came back in May.

A few days before my opening, we all went to Richard Harris's exciting concert in Lincoln Center. John and he had been discussing working together, and John has since become his manager as well. Richard and I did the "Johnny Carson Show" on March 30 and, I'm afraid, rather shamelessly plugged each other's openings throughout. That opening night was getting close. My daughters, Kirsa and Ana Maria, had arrived with Liz Marshall and Lois Musgrave, John's wife and secretary, from London, and my mother had flown in from Copenhagen. I was not short on moral support. (My son, Nicolas, had had women 'up to here' and had elected instead to go on holiday with a boy from school.) Walt, Derek and Jack had rehearsed with me to the point that I was about to suggest the billing be changed from "solo" to "quartet." The orchestra and the hotel, I knew, were rooting for me. Now came the crunch: what about everybody else?

Monday, April 3, was D-Day: Do or Die. I was nervous— no, I was terrified. My mother used to say when I was agonizing through final exams in high school, "They can't kill you,

11

so what are you afraid of?" In a literal sense of the word, I suppose they couldn't. John was buzzing like a bee, just as nervous as I, but he didn't let on, either. We had a full rehearsal that morning at eleven complete with TV films crews, and he was there in a bubbly mood trying to ease the strain for everyone while checking the lighting and sound systems just once more. There were press and photographers and other people—Lord knows who—rushing in and out, and the children sat on the edge of the stage watching, finally becoming restless and jumping at an invitation to go off to the zoo. *That* amused me, but otherwise I was oblivious to it all. I had a little note that day from Frederik—he knew what I was going through.

As I was in my room doing my makeup that evening, Sarah, the maid, came in. "You must read the 23rd Psalm before you go downstairs," she said in her Irish brogue, and I did. Roberto Vega of Elizabeth Arden came to put the finishing touches to my hair, as he'd do twice nightly for the next three weeks. It was the first time I'd indulged myself in such luxury: having mastered the art of arranging hairpieces down pat through years of touring, I usually just dunked my head under the bathtub tap. When I was ready I had my usual moment of quiet, then went down the service lift and the kitchen stairs (funny how they all look the same all over the world, however luxurious the hotel: dingy and drafty). I kept telling myself it was just another opening, but I had a hard time convincing myself that night. One of the things I always do to distract my mind from the immediate world around me is pace for an hour or so before going on stage: I've "mown" more carpets than I can count. But tonight both children slept in my room— there was no room for pacing. There were the three beds, then Kirsa's shoe shop: my fourteen pairs of shoes dragged from the cupboard and lined up in rows like soldiers; and then Ana Maria's stuffed animals—seven or eight of them—each tenderly bedded down on the floor wrapped in all the towels and bathmats she had pinched from our three bathrooms. Making one's way through all that was like playing leapfrog. I finally did my pacing in a little room downstairs, backstage.

12

From my seven new evening dresses, John, Donald Brooks and I had chosen one of the two blacks and a cock feather cape. Just before going on, Walt gave me a little mechanical clown who, when wound up, would clap the cymbals noisily together —just in case the applause was a bit thin. I hung my golden chain with my good-luck charms on him and (not being superstitious, knock wood) had him standing on the piano every night. (One night someone stole him between shows. The charms had no value except for me: a bit of amber, a piece of turquoise and my grandmother's little gold cross. That did upset me.) I could hear the orchestra tuning up and Jack was installing his harp. I had a moment of total panic. It lasted seconds, like a hot flash, and then I thought to myself, "I am going to go out there and just have a good time."—and I did.

Halfway through the first number I took off my cape and flung it at Walt—I can't remember if I missed or not (some nights I did). John had been back to wish me luck just before I went on and would now, I knew, be out there somewhere watching, white-faced, my every move and word. The white face was something I'd had to get used to when we started working together. The first time I ever saw him in the audience at London's Savoy (he usually stands in the back), he looked so upset that I completely lost my thread and gummed up the lyrics thinking something was terribly wrong. But not at all—he was only concentrating. Now he usually makes sure I can't see him.

Suddenly the show had come to an end. What had happened in between, I don't know, it had gone by so fast. I knew I'd done my best, and I was happy. It had been exciting, but I was also relieved—it was over with, for better or worse. I went up to change for the reception the St. Regis was hosting downstairs for the press and guests. The children were asleep, and I stood there looking at them for a long while, thinking to myself, "Well, things are beginning to look up a bit."

Then everybody started arriving in the suite: John, my mother, Liz, Lois, James (John's twin), Walt and Natalie Levinski, Jack and Derek and many more, and the merriment began. I was so happy for John—he'd worked so hard to make

13

the night a success. My mother cried as she always does when she's moved. I was glad she'd come, for the preceding months had been especially rough for her.

It was not until I saw the faces at the reception downstairs that I really knew everything was all right—it always takes a while to sink in.

There were congratulations and toasts and great animation. I chatted a bit with everyone, but suddenly felt terribly tired —the champagne on an empty stomach had made me a bit light-headed—and just wanted to escape. I quietly snuck off, soon followed by John, Liz and my mother. We bade each other a good night . . . and it was.

Earth Roots

I don't think I have any roots now, not even
in Ibiza, but I'll always have what I call "earth
roots." Sometimes, without warning, and in any spot in the
world, the lights or vegetation or the smell and sound of wind
rustling in pine trees will produce a terrible longing. It's not
for my home, my childhood house, which I can always see in
my memory or my mind, but it's some kind of earth root
feeling, something reminiscent of a place of peace, a place
known and familiar, a memory very distant. Perhaps it's a
throwback several centuries to my Scandinavian ancestors, all
very close to nature and really pagan at heart. Life was difficult
then and the people, especially in Norway, were very attuned
to the basic life forces about them, to the seasons, the rocks
and the mountains. It doesn't seem so strange then, that the
strongest memories of my own first years in Copenhagen are
of warmth and summer and greenery everywhere, all images,
colors and sounds rather than a replay of actual words or
conversations.

My parents had been married eleven years when I, their first
child, was born on July 15, 1932. My mother still laughs when
she recalls my father's arrival at the clinic that day.

"Here she is," said the private nurse, stopping Father in the corridor to show him the tiniest, most shriveled, blotchy pree-mie in the clinic. "That's a very bad joke," fumed the matron, stomping down the hall clutching the squalling baby—some-one else's.

Father opened the door to my mother's room and immedi-ately lost his glumness when he spotted me under a pink satin blanket and Mother in matching bow. "Of course," he ex-ulted, "she's beautiful!"

They'd met in England when Mother, Clara Undset Gyth, was attending finishing school and my father, Kaj Møller, was studying for the bar. He had English relatives and had always wanted to live there.

They both had been born in Denmark, she on Bastille Day, 1900, to a Danish father and Norwegian mother. One of six children (although three brothers died in childhood), she was raised in the undisturbed yet social privacy of a comfortable home. As with the generations before her and with my own until shortly after the war, there was the security of knowing life would go on much the way it always had. One married within one's own circle, raised the children to do the same and preserved the heritage and traditions of the family tree. It was a carefree upbringing. One's physical needs were taken care of by a staff of servants, leaving time to pursue the arts, music, languages, literature, travel and the development of one's character and sense of social responsibility.

As with all my earliest memories, my first recollections of Mother are more of impression than of specifics. I can't, for instance, remember one word of her admonitions on how to behave myself, but rather the total example she set for us in the conduct of her own life. She was and is a beautiful lady, who would cuddle me and stroke my brow at bedtime or hold my hand when I was ill, but whose stern authoritative voice was to be feared and respected when the house laws were broken. Yet, she always decked the breakfast table with pink roses and a flag for birthdays and worked most secretively behind closed living room and bedroom doors as Christmas drew near.

When she married shortly after her twenty-first birthday,

her shy beauty and natural graciousness were a perfect complement to my father's outgoing wit and brilliance. He was by then entitled to practice law in England, complete with black robes and tightly curled white wig, but never did. His father's death necessitated his returning to Copenhagen, where he took over with his brother the family-owned National Cash Register franchise. After a few years, he was offered the directorship of Denmark's largest conservative paper, *Berlingske Tidende*. He accepted and enthusiastically threw himself into his work, eventually founding the paper's successful magazine and book publishing divisions as well.

They had just moved into a large suburban home across the road from Prince Valdemar's castle, where the Czar's family used to visit, when they learned their first child would be born that summer. Father was especially jubilant. He immediately set to work designing a big nursery, so confident that his lifelong wish for a daughter was about to be granted that he did the whole thing in pinks and whites. In his enthusiasm, he also became an instant expert on what the traits of a top-notch nanny should be, interviewing, hiring and firing a whole string of them, even before the child had appeared. This continued after the great event, for at one point a few months later there were three nannies in residence: one just leaving, one just starting and a nurse to hold it all together. It was about that time that Mother, despite all the professional help, decided to take my temperature during a bout with a cold. Wanting to be sure the thermometer was clean beyond a doubt, she ran it under the hot water tap, then inserted it. The reading of 44.6 C. (138 F.) blew everyone's mind, and poor Mother fled the nursery in great haste!

Clearly I was the pride of my parents' existence. My layette was heavy with Belgian lace, my hand-embroidered shirts were from The White House in London, and I'd been carried home from the maternity clinic in complete triumph.

One of my earliest memories is the water stain on the ceiling of the nursery, a fascinating shape that, aided by the glow from the pink chintz curtains and the imagination of an almost-napping little child, turned into a horse, a swan, all sorts of marvelous fantasy things. And there was a Chinese wind chime hanging in the window, one of the nicest gifts I ever received.

The house itself—"Bernstorffslund"—was a happy, bustling place. Beyond the family, there were the servants: the nanny, maid, chauffeur, gardener and a very down-to-earth cook who, upon first seeing my mother's newly acquired authentic *Louis Seize* sofa, thought it terrible that her employers couldn't afford new furniture.

And there was the constant stream of guests. Because of my father's position and both parents' warm hospitality, the house was a favorite gathering place for artists and writers from the paper, members of the diplomatic corps and theatrical performers passing through town. The regular guests among these groups were always addressed as "Aunt" or "Uncle," and my very favorite "uncle" was Robert Storm Petersen, a satirical political cartoonist who worked with my father. In dressing gown and still-wet combed hair, I'd present myself and curtsy to the grown-ups during their before-dinner sherry. Uncle Storm would immediately launch into his incredible fairy tales of trolls and Danish household sprites, which are quite similar to Irish leprechauns. Then he'd lead me by the hand to all the dark nooks and crannies under the stairs and behind the furniture to show where they lived. I listened in wide-eyed fascination as he explained they were the Møller family fairies and would move with us wherever we went.

One afternoon, a friend of my mother visited with her West Indian maid, the first black I'd ever seen. I stared at her for many minutes, then asked out loud if I might touch her and, if so, would the color rub off on my hands. Needless to say, Mother was mortified and shushed me from the room as fast as possible.

When I think of the first Christmases, I remember the huge high-ceilinged and galleried library my father had built, for that's where the enormous tree always was placed. The Christmas celebration began with dinner on the twenty-fourth. At a beautifully decorated table (and Mother has never once repeated the Christmas table decor), a large group of family

18

and friends would first be served a cinnamon-flavored rice porridge topped with black currant juice and a big lump of butter. By tradition, in all the porridge there was one almond; whoever got it also received a special present. In truth, because none of us kids liked the porridge, there were always several almonds and several gifts. Then came the Christmas goose, just delivered by the baker's boy on his bicycle from the only ovens around big enough to hold the bird. It was a magnificent sight, complete with a Danish flag stuck into its back and served with red cabbage and apple and prune stuffing. Then the apple dumplings topped with strawberry jam were brought in. By that time, I was stuffed full, but no matter, for we all knew how delicious the cold dumplings would be at breakfast the next day.

When the doors of the library gallery were at last thrown open, we looked down on a breathtaking tree, at least ten to twelve feet high, completely lit with candles, and topped by a huge gold star. There were long strings of tiny Danish flags draped on its branches, chains of interwoven paper hearts, delicate handmade straw figures and ornaments, paper cones stuffed with licorice and, underneath, mountains of presents for everyone. We'd troop down the stairs—I was the smallest, but always the fastest—and march about the tree singing carols. At last the presents—and the "goodie table," a delicious spread of mandarins, oranges, figs, apples, dates, chocolates and a giant marzipan sausage sliced and served with coffee. Through all this, we children especially would check out the tree looking for favorite old decorations, some funny, some just lovely ornaments passed through the family, to make certain they'd not been lost during the year.

The twenty-fifth we were always at home to those relatives and friends who had not been with us the previous night. Despite the fun and more presents and a beautiful cold luncheon buffet, my stomach would draw into a knot thinking about Boxing Day, the twenty-sixth of December, and our traditional visit to my aunt's. It wasn't my aunt—she was lovely—but some of my male cousins who teased me unmercifully whom I dreaded. They were all older and much, much bigger than I, and delighted in chasing me about the house, then locking me in an unlit closet. I've always been afraid of the dark, so this was absolutely terrifying. Even worse, if I survived that, was their tickling me so badly that I almost wet my pants, and they still wouldn't stop.

My sister Susanne was born October 22, 1935, and not surprisingly, I was rather resentful of someone else stealing my limelight. I'm told I very matter-of-factly suggested to my parents that, since they already had me, they ought to give her to some people who didn't have any children. Happily, that was a short-lived attitude, and in spite of the usual childhood quarrels and the then drastic age difference, we always played together. Of course, *vis à vis* the grown-ups, we had the usual complaints and disdain for each other. "She's a bit tiresome," I used to say, "but then she's so much younger than I am!" Yet, when one was in trouble, the other always stood by in support.

My father created special entertainments for me with his shows of magic and sleight-of-hand. In my only clear-cut memory of him, I can still see his hands making feathers and flowers vanish into thin air, then suddenly reappear in the most unlikely places! Even more wondrous was his wrapping one black feather in a paper, then opening it to find five colored ones instead. I also was driven each afternoon by the chauffeur to my father's offices, where I'd march in by myself to fetch him home for dinner.

One night in the fall of 1936, I was awakened by a great commotion and flurry in the household, and the door between my room and my mother's was suddenly locked. Apparently, my parents had returned from dinner and my father had complained of not feeling well. When Mother walked back into the room with an aspirin, she found him on the bed dead from a heart attack. Although my four-year-old mind could not comprehend it all, I knew something terrible had happened and refused to eat. Mother sent me to stay with some close family friends whose daughter, Marita, already was a playmate of mine (and is now my oldest friend).

A short while later, Mother found the empty, memory-filled

house unbearable and rented a cottage in the hills above Monte Carlo. It was a small pink house, just big enough for her, the nanny and us, and was surrounded by orange trees, the first I'd ever seen. For some reason, I can still see that house as clearly in my mind's eye as if I'd been there yesterday, and would be able to find it immediately if I were to return today. The nanny was a beautiful Norwegian who, Mother says, strongly resembled Ingrid Bergman and was very much sought after by the young men of the area. Next door lived the Casino's doorman, whose children became our playmates and taught me fluent French. Unfortunately, I eventually forgot it all and, years later when I lived in Paris, was miserable until I relearned the language from scratch.

When next we moved to Rapallo, my maternal grandmother came to stay with us. A fascinating woman, she was regal in her long dresses with stay-supported collars and beaded ruching, high-button boots and a black walking stick. In her capacious handbag, there always were lots of little boxes full of candies, pastilles and chewing gum, through which Sussi and I were allowed to rummage as a special treat. Her fairy tales were awesome. After reading us all the Hans Christian Andersen and Grimm Brothers stories, she'd relate tales of the "Nisser," the playful red-capped "Little People," and the horrendous Norwegian trolls. Her descriptions of the trolls' wickedness were scary, but each time she came to visit us over the years, I couldn't wait to hear more. As I think about them now, children's fairy tales are more gruesome and filled with more mayhem, murders, neck-breakings and all-round violence than all the B-movies and tabloid papers lumped together.

Once on a visit from Rapallo to her home in Rome, she took us in a cart driven by a hackman named Federico and pulled by Rosa, his old mare, to the Catacombs and the Quo Vadis Chapel. There, with great solemnity, she explained the special significance of a large footprint set in stone, supposedly that of St. Peter. After pondering someone's ability to make a footprint in *stone,* all I could blurt out in the hush of the chapel was, "But, how much did he weigh?"

During the time we spent south, Mother never revealed her sorrow but always seemed her lovely self, going for rides in horse buggies, taking us to the beach and trying to preserve the happiness we'd known in Copenhagen. Her grief was a very private thing, which no one saw nor heard, an example of the emotional self-control she instilled in my sister and me from our earliest days. Then and for many years after, I never felt a sense of deprivation in not having a father as my friends did, but rather a sadness that I could never really know him. Hearing from Mother and their friends how brilliant and amusing and creative he'd been gave me both a sense of pride and a very real deep ache. I painted an idealistic fantasy picture of him in my mind, long certain that if he'd been there, he surely would have taken my side in arguments with my mother. And we did argue, sometimes almost violently, but I've still always loved, admired and respected her more than anyone in the world.

We returned to the house in Copenhagen and the world of the nursery, ruled by nannies whose stern decisions could rarely be overturned by appeals to my mother. Our meals were served there, we slept there and, except for long summer hours in the garden and school when we were old enough, lived there amidst toys and books and crisply starched servants. Our food was brought in on trays, with personally monogrammed silver soup plates, mugs and utensils (all traditional christening gifts), and a strange instrument simply called a "pusher-upper," for getting things onto your fork in lieu of a knife. Fingers in this case were unthinkable!

The nannies wore starched uniforms with starched aprons and collars and gold pins indicating which nanny school they'd attended. The food was very good, although I remember deliberately spitting out great gushes of the much-detested spinach onto all that ordered neatness. The next meal, another bowl of it was served, and this continued until I ate it without fuss or complaint. This occurred with other unfavorite foods as well. Once I even went on a hunger strike for three days to make the nanny feel sorry for forcing me to eat some dreadful thing—liver, probably. But nannies are tough, and it was I who folded, ravenously agreeing to eat *anything*. We'd visit the cook whenever there were special things going on in the kitchen, like jam cooking, baking for Christmas and, best of all, when we'd be having eel for dinner and the cook would chase the writhing thing all around with a meat cleaver.

It was a peaceful, secure existence. The only real unpleasantness was our beds, iron-hard chromium contrivances that pulled out to accommodate our growth. They were made even more Spartan by pillows that were flat horsehair mats, good for posture development, Mother said. As we grew taller, the beds seemed more and more uncomfortable, thus my great joy to receive as a confirmation gift at age thirteen a real honest-to-goodness bed on which appeared, as if by magic, a pillow stuffed with real feathers! There were also chromium bars on the windows of both our rooms to keep us from falling out—my room, larger than Sussi's and thus the playroom as well, was in a tower. For some reason, even after we'd passed the falling-out stage, they were never removed and were still there when we moved.

Our greatest nursery activity—Sussi's and mine—was plotting our strategies against the nannies. At times—oh joy!—we succeeded in reducing one to tears, but then immediately felt so rotten about it that we cried, too. One nanny was "The Manor Lady" because of her very regal appearance. Another we called "The Holy Ghost" (behind her back, of course), due to her habit of conducting elaborate prayer sessions any time the spirit moved her, which was much too often for our liking. Another nanny, a rather glamorous Swedish widow, added much to our secular education by sunbathing nude in the rose garden, often joined by the chauffeur. Supposedly napping, we would instead sit up behind our chromium bars giggling, trying to figure out what they were up to. Actually, there wasn't that much involved—they mostly reminded me of the statues I'd seen on museum trips with a best friend and her grandfather.

The best world of all for me, though, was the garden, quite extensive even to the adult eye. All along one side, from the library to the back of our property, ran a covered, tree-formed

23

alley we called a pergola. Near this and just behind the hot-house was the large, multicolored rose garden partially ring-ing two small ponds connected by a narrow irrigation canal. Here we'd try to catch the goldfish and tadpoles with butterfly nets and, occasionally, "exile" a particularly nasty playmate or two. For this, we'd lay the gardener's ladder across one of the ponds to a small rock in the middle, dupe the unsuspecting child onto it, then pull back the ladder and leave him stranded until his or our nanny retrieved him.

The beautifully tended flower beds all about the main lawn were planted so that there was a constantly changing mass of color from winter's end through the first severe fall frost. One of the terraces was edged in great clouds of lavender, always in bloom just in time for us to make in great secrecy (and with Nanny's help and ragbag) sachets for Mother's birthday.

Next to the pond with the fountain in the middle was an old white Italian marble bench, on which I'd dream and play with my dolls for hours. But my very favorite spot, in a grove of pines, was my giant fern, the perfect hideaway for a shy child with an active imagination. I'd crawl into it and just sit, fanta-sizing about the elves and sprites who surely lived amongst all those flowers and trees and quite smug that no one, save the Little People themselves, knew where I was. All of this—the carefully raked paths, the arbors, the stands of birch and wil-lows, azaleas and rhododendrons, the tennis courts, the whole outdoor scene—was presided over by Mr. Olsen, the gar-dener. He loathed kids and would shudder, then shout, if any ventured near his beds and bushes. In the make-believe world of a six-year-old, he was undoubtedly the closest thing to a flesh-and-blood troll extant!

Right next to our house was a riding school and stable, then the large, forbidding, ivy-covered house of an old lady whom we never saw. In a three-room apartment in one wing of that house, though, lived another lady, very tall and thin, with flaming red hair bound up with bright gypsy scarves. She had dozens of cats and dogs and raised every type of vegetable and flower imaginable in the old lady's garden. Many summer evenings after my bath and dinner, I'd run through the hedge

24

and across the road in my nightclothes to join the "gypsy lady" on her evening walk. Patiently, she'd explain all the secrets of nature, how funny-looking dry bulbs became lovely flowers, how to tell one bird or duck egg from another by their shapes and colors as they lay in the nests in the grass, how the trees and flowers knew when it was time each spring to come to life. She understood so much about nature and really opened my eyes to a fascinating experience. Being eaten alive by the swarms of mosquitos was just a small part of the whole thing.

Equally fascinating, but not nearly so desirable in our nanny's eyes, were what we kids thought were the "impoverished families," who lived in much simpler style in the old lady's other wing. One of the children there, Peter, was our special friend. He looked like a street urchin with his nose forever running, and his straw-yellow hair so stiff with grime and grease that our nanny was convinced he had lice. Sussi and I were secretly envious of him because he somehow had figured out a way to get out of bathing or shampooing his hair at all. For us, that was a too-frequent and arduous process, complete with raw eggs and vinegar rinses. Sussi was lucky, for she had short hair and bangs, but hair washings for me also meant rolling damp hair in pink silk ribbons. For years I had to sleep on those hateful lumpy knots, then endure a brisk early-morning brushing to produce ringlets. Eventually comfort was acknowledged and I was allowed to have braids.

We had great fun with Peter visiting the stables, chasing the ducks around the old lady's pond—and supplying his family with loo paper. His amazement at the idea of having loo paper on rolls instead of stacks of torn newspaper horrified us. So, we'd smuggle the stuff out to him from our guest bath at garden level, Sussi pulling yards of it out the window while I furtively unrolled it from inside, with the door carefully locked.

Each spring I'd plant my own little garden in a patch next to the tennis courts. With money saved from my allowance, I'd buy paper seed packets with beautiful pictures on the outside of what was going to come up. With my own watering can, I faithfully tended that patch, waiting anxiously for flowers and vegetables to appear. At last there'd be two or three sickly sprouts separated from each other by an immense, healthy sea of weeds. Still, every spring my hope returned, never diminished by the failure of the year before. One thing that did survive was a foot-high birch tree I planted when I was only about five or six years old. By the time we moved in 1946, it was well over six feet tall. It was quite sad to say goodbye to that tree, for we'd grown up together and were very special friends. I used to chatter encouragements to it and sit under it early each spring and summer morning on my before-school tours of the garden. I also was the unofficial "flower inspector," always checking to see what new flowers—especially tulips—had burst open. They've always been my favorite flower and Mr. Olsen had planted hundreds of every variety and color. When he wasn't looking, I'd stick my fingers into some of them to collect the dew and purple dust to make nanny-shocking tattoos on my arms.

The calla lilies were the one thing in the garden I hated, maybe because my mother had once told me they were funeral flowers and looked beautiful on gravesites. Growing in a long, depressing bed on the shaded north side of the high hedge, their tall, stern stalks seemed cold and forbidding. Flowers should be such joyous creations, not instruments for saying goodbye! I did like the three potted palms which sat on the terraces in the warm months, then were moved to the hothouse off the library in the winter. The hothouse was marvelously warm and steamy, a great place to play in spite of the few toads and the one caution-inspiring snake (I hate snakes!) there to keep the balance of nature in line. There were small clusters of grapes, too, but cleverly hung just high enough to escape our reach.

I had begun first grade at the coeducational Ordrup Private School shortly after our return from Rapallo and Rome. That first day, I went off with the chauffeur and car and a great deal of trepidation. Already aware of Mother's very high ideals for me, I was terribly afraid I'd not measure up to her standards and not please my teacher and the rest of the family. Besides that, I was a very shy child, quite fearful of having to face that whole new world head-on and alone. But the small classes, finding new friends and being in a small schoolhouse instead of a colder, more conventional building resolved my fears, and I began to like it and did well.

That winter Mother took us skiing in Kitzbuhel in the Austrian Alps. As much fun as it was to be with her on such an outing, it was also where I suffered my first truly humiliating experience with the opposite sex. We'd been out on the slopes for hours in the bitter cold, but I was too timid to interrupt the adults with a simple physical need. The result was I wet my pants, soaking right through all the layers of underthings to the ski outfit itself. As I tried to avoid looking at a dashing young seven-year-old with whom I'd been shyly flirting earlier, my pants froze—solid. How mortifying! This six-year-old temptress now resembled nothing so much as a wishbone in mittens.

Later, warm and drowsy and blissfully thawed out, I stood in our hotel room window and watched ranks of soldiers move past in a strange, stiff-legged march, as if their pants had frozen, too. I couldn't understand the grown-ups' not sharing my excitement for this living marionette-show performance— only years later did I realize I'd been a witness to the *Anschluss*.

The following winter, our dining room resembled a warehouse, piled high with crates of bandages, cottons and hundreds of skeins of gray wool. Our house had become the meeting place for Mother's Red Cross circle busily sewing, knitting and making first aid kits for the soldiers in the Finnish-Russian War. Of course I had to join in, painstakingly turning my very first knitting effort into an oddly shaped, hole-ridden gray muffler. The nanny would pick up dropped stitches, the chauffeur stood patiently each evening as I measured the day's work on his neck, and I was thrilled by the romantic notion of this splendid scarf saving some poor Finnish soldier from freezing to death.

In the spring of 1940, I was to see more companies of German soldiers, this time right in the streets of Copenhagen. We'd been skiing again with Mother, this time in Gola, Norway. For some reason, although her Danish friends there

27

urged her to extend the holiday, she adamantly refused. We returned to Copenhagen April 7 and checked into the elegant old landmark hotel, The Cosmopolite, to await the reopening of our own home. The same day our new nanny arrived. Miss Bay had been born in Denmark but raised in England, and her linguistic abilities in Danish were nil. We were to learn English, Mother had decided, and after a conference in the bathroom (the only place one could lock the door), my sister and I decided this had great possibilities. Through sign language we could tell Miss Bay all sorts of tales of how things had been run in the past and, of course, pretend not to understand her at all when she gave an order.

That night and the next when she took us to the hotel's starched and red plush dining room, the place was almost filled with tables of somber, rather stiff German traveling salesmen. They nodded formally and smiled only barely at our two little blonde heads as we passed by to our table. The evening of the eighth, Mother dined at the Uruguayan Embassy and later I remember her, very serious-faced, receiving many phone calls and worried visitors all in very hush-hush tones. The next morning, April 9, 1940, the German salesmen were suddenly German officers. Their "sample cases" had carried but one sample—their full military regalia. We learned from leaflets dropped from German planes flying over the capital that troops were pouring in over the Jutland border and from ships in Copenhagen harbor. If we did not surrender immediately, Copenhagen would be leveled. The Occupation had begun.

By late morning, we were packed up and ready to go home, but all the joy had gone out of finally returning to our garden and toys, and all the grown-ups had tears in their eyes. As we rode through the streets of Copenhagen, we passed lots of cars and people on bicycles fleeing the city in fear of the bombs, which never fell. But our house and garden were still the same as when we'd last seen them, and it was hard to believe the outside world was quite topsy-turvy. We didn't know then that Denmark, like the rest of Europe, would be under the German yoke for the next five years.

A day or two later, Norway was invaded, and our Danish

28

friends who had remained at Gola were forced to flee through Russia and then to America, where they spent the entire war as refugees. We were glad to be in our own home, no matter what. . . .

War Years

The first two years of the Occupation changed very little of our—the children's—lives, except the grown-ups looked more serious and Miss Bay had learned Danish. The first of May, summer was announced as usual by the reappearance of white ankle socks and cotton dresses, the bringing out of the lawn furniture to be repainted, and Mr. Klausen's arriving to clean the crystal chandeliers. For this, he set up two stepladders in the rock garden behind the library, ran a pole between them and hung each chandelier from that. Very carefully he would take off the rows of crystals looking like a giant's necklace, tenderly wash and dry them till they sparkled in the sun, then reassemble the whole thing, while we watched in fascination. Carpets and cushions were brought out to be bashed with wicker beaters, furniture polished and curtains washed until the whole house smelled of soap and spring air.

Beyond the confines of "Bernstorffslund" things were not so different yet, either. The official German propaganda line was that the Occupation of Denmark had been done solely as a "defense measure." Unlike their defense measures in Norway and Holland, where they'd had to fight every step of the way, the Germans had met only small border skirmishes in

Jutland before taking over the entire country. Our national administrative institutions—the utilities and public services—were allowed to go on as before, under German supervision, of course, and even the army was permitted to stay in the same garrisons.

There were no German regiments marching through the countryside. In fact, the only times I saw their green uniforms those first months were when Mother took me into the main part of Copenhagen. Quite a few people felt a sense of shame that Denmark hadn't resisted the invasion more as our Dutch and Norwegian cousins had, despite their heavy losses. However, when the Danish underground got into action, the world —and certainly the invaders—knew we'd just begun to retaliate.

Petrol was one of the first shortages, so our car was put on wooden blocks and the chauffeur slowly relegated to household duties, much to his dismay. People became quite ingenious in their means of transportation, and it was not unpleasant the way the frantic pace of life slowed down. Friends began arriving in the afternoon for tea by horse and carriage or bicycle. I can still see the carts in the drive and the horses tethered to the clothes lines behind the garage, calmly chewing on the dish towels and some other strange knitted objects. Those were always a mystery to us kids, and our questions brought very vague replies. Years later, I discovered they were our cook's hand-crocheted sanitary napkins!

My grandmother was not to be denied her visits, so she arrived by pedal taxi, that is, a little plywood wagon hitched to a bicycle, a service run mainly by students. How lucrative it was compared to the energy expended, I don't know. Eventually, even commercial trucks were forced to rely on small wood or peat-burning stoves to keep them going.

Food rationing was the initial effect the children felt from the Occupation. The Germans early on began shipping Danish farm produce out of the country to feed their own people and troops, though they did the unforgivable thing to us of never rationing vegetables. Imports of exotic foods, raw materials for manufacturers and even everyday goods had slowed down.

Coffee and tea were among the first to go, and a Dane without coffee for his pastry was a sorry enough sight until butter and sugar joined the list. Marzipan, another Danish staple, was now made of mashed potatoes sweetened with saccharin and coated with a thin layer masquerading as chocolate, but really paraffin with a phony chocolate taste. It was ghastly, but we ate it! We used to buy paraffin at the apothecary and, with oodles of spit and much determined chewing, it would eventually stick together. Then a squidge of toothpaste for flavor, and voilá—chewing gum! It was kept in a glass of water overnight and next morning you started the whole procedure over again.

My playmates and I secretly used to hoard bits of butter and sugar from our respective kitchens, store them all week in cool cellar niches, then gather Saturdays in an otherwise unoccupied kitchen with windows wide open to dissipate the giveaway smell and make the best caramel and fudge I'd ever tasted.

Despite the annoyance of rationing, none of the children I knew ever felt a real sense of deprivation. I had been born not with a silver spoon, necessarily, though certainly a very pleasant spoon and was, in many ways, spoiled materially. But, I was equally spoiled with love, something I see sadly lacking in many children's upbringing today. They appear to be granted every material wish as a love substitute, but how can a lonely child snuggle up to an over-crammed toy chest? We certainly did *not* get everything we wanted, and saved our small allowances for some object without which we surely would perish. (Usually, by the time we'd gotten enough money together to buy it, our interest had died altogether and we were already dreaming of something else.) Today, Christmas and birthdays seem to mean so little to children, for in many homes, it's Christmas all year round. There aren't the months of hope and anticipation we knew, wondering in a delicious agony if the thing we wanted most would be under the tree or on the birthday breakfast table.

We were always taken into the center of Copenhagn on King Christian X's birthday, September 26, and this year the

32

celebration was especially meaningful. Sussi and I wore Danish national costumes and joined tens of thousands of Danes waving their flags in salute to His Majesty. I recall once seeing him ride on a huge white horse down the middle of one of Copenhagen's main streets. This he did everyday and continued to do all through the war. There was no mistaking that tall, bony-structured figure—it *was* the King. As he passed, I curtsied deeply as I'd been taught to do in respect to all my elders and certainly to him. He smiled and saluted. A minute or so later, he rode past a German soldier who drew himself to attention. King Christian's face became a piece of granite. He looked neither right nor left, just continued the slow, defiant ride alone through his city.

He was greatly loved by his people and was a special symbol of inspiration and defiance of the Germans. When the rumors began circulating that the Germans would compel all Danish Jews to wear yellow armbands to separate them from the rest of the population, the King was furious. In his eyes, all his subjects were *Danes,* nothing more, nothing less. He let it be known that, if the order were effected, *he* would be the first to don the armband. The Germans backed down, and neither the Danish nor Norwegian Jews ever had to endure that humiliation.

School continued normally, and I liked it, except for two things: a red-headed class bully who, accompanied by his gang, took special delight in ambushing me as I was leaving, and would play cat-and-mouse with me on his bicycle until he knocked me off mine. My defense system was to park my bicycle in such a way that I could get out before he did, and my triumph was indescribable the day I managed to let the air out of his tires and pedal off furiously as he stood there fuming. My other problem was Miss Rump, meaning "ass" in Danish, a name I thought she well deserved.

She was a tall, thin scarecrow of a woman with the traditional knot of greasy gray hair tied in a bun at the back of her head and clouds of dandruff on the back of her long shapeless print dresses. If we didn't know our sums, she'd stalk up and down the classroom aisles either thumping our heads with a thimble she always wore on her right hand or pulling the tiny hairs on our temples. To see those spindly legs clad in baggy brown wool stockings and "sensible" shoes coming my way was truly fearsome. One morning in her class as long division was going especially badly, I suddenly felt quite ill—oh, what a relief at that point—and she sent me home. My whole body felt so weak that I couldn't ride my bicycle but had to walk it along the street instead.

I was sent to bed immediately and stayed there for a month, constantly vomiting and growing weaker day by day, and subsisting only on rose hip tea. No one could figure out what was wrong with me. One afternoon I suddenly felt marvelous —no pain, no nausea—quite like floating on a big pink cloud. I was vaguely aware of Mother's putting cool cloths on my hands, feet and face, and the doctor's bending over me. My strange illness had finally been diagnosed as para-dysentery, and he wasn't sure I could be saved. The theory was that I had been infected by the horses while feeding them grapes I had stolen from the hothouse. It took me twenty years to eat a grape again. In the rush to the hospital, though, the fever miraculously broke. The private night nurse my mother had hired, a fat lady with big whiskers (I wasn't so ill not to notice), assured me I only had to ask for anything I wanted. Within minutes, she'd settled herself into a chair across the room and was snoring with the buzzing of a sawmill. Several times I desperately wanted some water, but my arms were too weak to reach the carafe and I was too shy to wake her. And, of course, her performance which might have been restorative for her, kept me awake all night. Finally after three nights of this, but still not wanting to rat on her, I told my mother I didn't think I needed her anymore and she was dismissed.

Because of the contagion factor, Mother was the only visitor permitted, and then only after donning a white sterile gown. She always came at mealtimes, hoping to cheer me on as I faced the latest bowl of lumpy oatmeal porridge *sans* milk, salt or sugar. She read to me all five volumes of the Hans Christian Andersen stories from a beautiful red and blue leather-bound set sent by a family friend. The books had to stay on a table

34

across the room from my bed, for anything I touched could not leave the hospital. The only other "company" I had was a little boy whom I never saw. His sweet, pure singing of nursery rhymes at any time of night or day used to float in from his nearby room. One day the singing stopped. He had died early that morning, the Matron said, and I cried secretly under my blankets for my unseen friend.

It was about that time that I first had a disturbing nightmare that still comes back to haunt me. It begins with my being chased through a great swamp, my pursuer's feet making giant suction-cup noises as he races after me through the hot, fetid bog. Gradually it dissolves into a dream of conscious imagery in which I see my body breaking up into small square pieces, which my mind and will vainly try to get back together again. This nightmare has recurred several times both during illness and emotionally problematic times. I wonder what it means. . . .

Discharge from the hospital was not to the old familiar nursery, but to Vestersøhus, a private hotel in Copenhagen. Coal was in such short supply now that heating the big house was impossible, so for the next three or four winters, we'd move bag and baggage into town.

Sussi, who changed school with me the following year, and I were not at all unhappy about these arrangements, for we would then be able to walk to school. Ice skating on the old city moat and the nearby lake plus visits to the swim baths were so much easier, too.

Roller skating when weather permitted was practiced in the long paved yard running along the back of the block. But, this was rough on the hated long woolen stockings, which were getting scarce. We all hoped they might disappear altogether, but no such luck. They were mended and mended, until the knees turned into pads of multi-shaded brown yarn scars.

As at home, there was always a constant parade of pets moving in and out. Some lived out their allotted span, but others vanished disastrously, like the goldfish which, having been dumped into the loo by my sister for what she thought was a much-needed shower, never appeared again after she

35

pulled the chain. We also had a family of mice which grew by leaps and bounds, much to our delight. Nevertheless, it *was* an accident when one day Mother mistook the newest litter for scraps of uneaten sausage, swept sawdust, micelets and all into the loo and, again, the chain was pulled. The mother mouse departed soon after, courtesy of a slammed door, and for that we were allowed a day off from school for mourning.

Another advantage to living in town, at least in our eyes, were the few air raid alerts. That's when we got to pack up our dolls and, wrapped up in appropriate woolies, head for the basement. There we sat on wooden benches, under a blue-tinted bulb giving everyone a ghostly look, and hoped it would last and last so we wouldn't have to go to bed.

At home, our favorite playgrounds on rainy days were the attic full of secret passages and shelves and the basement in which my father had built a theatre for his and his friends' amusement. In the attic one day we found a huge parcel of long thin strips of beautiful silk—strangely colored, we thought, in its brown and green spots. We distributed the strips to all our girl-friends, and within two days every doll and stuffed animal on the street was beautifully attired in the mysterious silk. It turned out it was the first camouflage parachute dropped by the Allies after the Occupation. My mother had a terrible time rounding up all the bits and pieces missing before anybody got wind of what it was.

That summer someone got the idea of crocheting beanies or skull-caps in the red, white and blue insignia of the RAF. Within days, everybody had crocheted and was wearing this emblem, much to the fury of the Germans who immediately outlawed it.

For years Mother had had quite a few suitors, all of whom were keenly dissected in private by my sister and me, categorized quite neatly as to the sizes of gifts they brought us and the degree of warmth with which Mother greeted them. There was one eccentric gentleman in particular who was *really* in our favor. He always arrived long after bedtime with the most incredible presents, not because it was Christmas or our birthdays, but just because he liked bringing us gifts. One

36

summer night around ten o'clock, we were hauled out of bed by the nanny. Into the nursery came this suitor's chauffeur, uniform and all, carrying a six-foot-long dollhouse and three or four boxes of furniture and accessories for it. Its donor was obviously the top contender in the "stepfather stakes" in our greedy little eyes. However, we had noticed there were often phone calls from one person with whom my mother always spoke in an especially tender voice, but his telephone voice matched none of the gentlemen who came to the house. Greatly intrigued by this, we carefully scrutinized the Christmas gifts which filled her room long before the holidays. The monograms on a special pile of things to one side matched none of the names on our "working list," and no name had been tagged on. Finally, one spring morning in 1943, Mother called us in to her bedroom, took a photograph from beneath her pillow and told us that she was to marry my godfather, Hugo Helms Hasselbalch. We heartily approved of Mother's choice—we'd always known him and loved him dearly. He was in the throes of a divorce, the complications of which were to last until 1946 when finally they were married.

July we spent at Skagen, the northernmost point of Jutland, where the North Sea meets the Skagerak. The entire west coast at this point had been heavily fortified by the Germans with bunkers, barbed wire and steel anti-tank contraptions. Despite the heavily mined sea, the fishermen still went out and one day brought back in their catch the bloated body of a German soldier, which we watched with horror being hoisted ashore.

That summer, with meat rationing already severe, we learned to love fish. Speaking of food, we spent our midterm holiday on the island of Bornholm, later to be the only part of Denmark liberated by the Russians. This was my first venture in an airplane, a small, prewar two-propellered machine, nonpressurized, with seats for eight. On Bornholm, the mushroom crop was unbelievable, and obviously had not been cleaned out for some time. Apparently the German soldiers on their forays into the woods did not know the difference between the poisonous and non-poisonous mushrooms and had

37

paid their price. So, we arrived each night back at the hotel with basketsful.

The Army and Navy personnel were interned in August of 1943, and the Germans took over the infantry barracks near our home. There began a night and day patrol of three soldiers walking up and down our road. Our reaction to them was the old inbred hatred, but I remember sometimes feeling sorry for them. They probably had children our own age and always tried to smile and nod to us as we went sweeping by on our bicycles, totally ignoring them, of course.

My mother felt very strongly that, as a widow with the sole responsibility of two children, she could not participate actively in the underground. However, she would support it financially and open the house to people who had to go into hiding or needed a way-station en route to Sweden. That fall the house constantly saw the coming and going of cousins and friends, but such social bustle was not new to us. One day, though, Mother called Sussi and me into the bathroom, locked the door and, while she fixed her hair, turned very serious, saying, "You are not to discuss at school or tell any of your friends about people who visit or stay at this house. Some of them are on the run from the Germans, and if they ever find out we are housing them, they will take me away and I shall be shot or sent to prison. You will never see me again. Do you understand?" We understood. To the day of liberation, we both kept our secrets and never betrayed her confidence.

With morbid fascination and horror, we heard dinner guests tell of a friend of my mother's in whose home the Germans had found explosives. They gave her ten minutes to get out before blowing up the whole place, the standard penalty for this crime—antiques, priceless oil paintings, the works. The only thing she grabbed was her unanswered mail. We learned of a well-loved "aunt" whom we hadn't seen for some time. She had been receiving ammunition dumped by the RAF onto her estate, lying in the fields herself at night to get it, then transport it to preassigned places. She'd been caught and condemned to death, the first woman in Denmark to incur the death penalty. Her only reaction upon hearing the sentence was to calmly powder her nose. The sentence was commuted to life imprisonment, and she was sent to Germany where she died.

Christmas that year saw friends and relatives missing, but we received one Christmas card which really cheered us up. It was from my mother's brother who, being in the Intelligence Service, had gone underground and allegedly was in England. This confirmed the rumor. Although the stamp was Danish, the card inside depicted a Christmas tree under which were shells marked "From Uncle Joe Stalin," crates marked "Ammunition to Danish patriots from John Bull," and boxes of rifles tagged "From Uncle Sam." The *pièce de résistance* of the card, the main greeting of which was "Merry Christmas from The Allies," was a figure of Adolph Hitler swinging from a noose on a candlelit branch.

One morning bicycling to the station to take the train to school, my sister and I passed by a huge brown stain on the pavement partially covered with flowers. We stopped and ran into the milk shop nearby to ask what had happened. The Germans, in reprisal for the underground's killing of an informer, had shot a prominent member of the community and dropped him there. That became the grim but common practice of the small "korps" organized by the Germans and made up of sadistic Danish felons and collaborators. They and the Gestapo were the nightly terror of important and prominent citizens, bursting into homes with no warning and machine gunning their victims in their beds as wives and children looked on.

Thinking back, it was curious that we never played "Germans and Patriots." There were just as many boys as girls on our road, all of whom had read *Robin Hood*, *The Three Musketeers* and all of James Fenimore Cooper's Indian tales. Most of our childhood games were patterned on these adventures. But, when the boys beheaded all our dolls à la *The Scarlet Pimpernel*, we didn't think *"Liberté, Égalité, Fraternité"* was that attractive any more. At that time, I had a mad crush on a boy down the road, but in his eyes, I was merely another victim to be tied to trees and down whose dresses worms and toads

39

just had to be dropped. Funny, times don't really change that much. . . .

The Germans had, of course, taken over the newspapers (including *Berlingske Tidende*), filling them with lies and propaganda. Within the next year, the front pages would consist of lists of those either arrested and/or condemned to death or those who had already been executed. The only way we could learn the truth was through the underground newspaper, slipped through the mail slot at five in the morning, and the B.B.C. broadcasts in Danish. We'd listen each night with the nanny to these programs that always included coded "greetings," indicating that night's dumping locations for ammunition and returning members of the underground.

Hardly a night went by that spring that the underground didn't seriously harass the Germans through sabotage. In June the Danish collaborators, on German orders, blew up Tivoli Gardens, and that really registered with me and my friends. Street skirmishes between the Danes and the Germans began and, on June 26, 1944, the Germans imposed a curfew from 8:00 P.M. to 5:00 A.M. Skirmishes continued. On June 30 the Germans finally provoked the Danes into a general strike, and street fights ensued in which many people were killed or wounded. Food was hoarded, and the shops closed down when shelves had been emptied. Water was stored in family bathtubs. That evening, German troops took over the gas, electric and water works, and all of Denmark came to a standstill. The Danes were ready to fight and threw up barricades all over town, while the exodus of the civilian population, lasting all through the weekend, began. Meanwhile, the Germans and the Danish government negotiated. We weren't allowed to stray far from the house and anxiously pounced upon anyone returning from central Copenhagen for the latest news. When unrest finally settled down for a while, Mother sent us off to my aunt and uncle, who had a large country estate in the south of Fyn. The place was called Rødkilde, "red spring" in Danish, so named because the natural spring on the property had a very high iron content.

My uncle had the most intriguing name of Baron Johan

Schaffalitzky de Muckadell, which was of Polish origin. He was a stern but gentle man with ramrod straight posture probably stemming from his time in the cavalry. With the house full of visitors and children all summer, he had set down very strict rules for meal and bed times. We were summoned by a bugle and woebetide the ones who were late, yet he never raised his voice. All he had to do was look at us and order was instantly restored. He was always just and fair and we really loved and respected him. He was also extremely active in the underground, but we never knew this, of course.

The main house had been built in the mid-nineteenth century. There were long rows of airy salons with French windows curtained in thin transparent material that billowed in the breeze, faded chintzes on the sofas, family portraits on the walls, and floors either of scrubbed oak or painted pale gray, very reminiscent of the country houses in Ingmar Bergman's pictures. Few of these rooms were ever used, as everybody usually gathered in the library or on the terrace during the warm summer evenings. We would watch the peacocks prancing up and down, go off after dinner to shoot rats in the old water mill and, on very clear dark nights, we could see the southern sky turn yellow (another heavy bombardment of the northern parts of Germany). The stable buildings with thatched roofs enclosed a cobblestone yard in the center of which was a lawn with a flagpole. Many early mornings one could find some unpopular youth's underwear and pants flying from the pole. By the time the hapless victim had retrieved his things, we would be long gone.

There was also a huge water trough for the animals, into which we dived every morning. The water was neck high and icy cold, but none of us would admit to less physical fitness than that of Uncle Johan, who marshaled the bathers each morning. After that we were all over the farm riding haywagons, milking cows, stealing apples from the orchard, playing in the barn, chasing the pigs when no one was watching, bicycling to the beach—a long sweaty haul—or having naval battles on the pond in the huge wooden laundry tubs. There was a tame goose called Gaekkemand who used to waddle up

41

the sweeping main staircase and tap on the front door. Eventually, his boldness brought him into the house and made him a general nuisance. He eventually went the way of all good chickens and naughty geese, namely under the axe. He was even served up for dinner, but that night we all went on strike.

My aunt Else was a lovely fragile lady, always very pale and wearing big straw hats to keep the sun from her skin. She was usually quiet and soft-spoken, but at family festivities when Danish tradition requires an endless amount of speeches, hers, done totally ex tempore, were always in verse and certainly the most beautiful. Sadly, they were never written down. She suffered frequently from migraine headaches and her delicate health did not permit her to sit through my uncle's cheese ritual after a plentiful country lunch. This entailed the maid's bringing in a large glass dome under which was the smelliest piece of yellow cheese loaded with maggots. We all stayed glued to our chairs in fascination as my uncle would slice the cheese and maggots in half and, without batting an eye, consume it, then turn to a round of applause from all the kids.

I never knew how many rooms there were at Rødkilde. However, there were only two bathrooms, which went by the stately names of The White Countess and The Brown Countess. Except for the fact that each was done in the color suggested and contained the old-fashioned ornate throne, I do not know the origin of these nicknames. The old buildings were National Trust landmarks, but in 1949 everything except the main house burned to the ground. It was a flash fire. None of the livestock could be saved, and the screams of the cattle and the smell of burned flesh were to haunt my aunt and uncle forever. The stables were rebuilt in efficient modern style, but not long afterward they sold the property and moved to town —I think my uncle just lost heart. He has since died, but Aunt Else still lives in Copenhagen.

On September 19 the air raid alert was suddenly blown at 11:00 A.M. It didn't last long, as I remember, but shortly after my mother arrived and without explanation took us home even before school was out. The reason, we found out later, was that the Germans, now wanting complete control over the country, had decided to remove the police. In a clever ruse, they had staged an air raid, knowing only the police were allowed on the street at such times. They had been rounded up easily and were en route to concentration camps by nightfall. Two of those who escaped soon enlarged our household "staff": one became the chauffeur, a rather ludicrous position considering there were no cars. His cover name was William, and he used to do my English lessons with me each afternoon. The other became the gardener but was shortly sent on to Sweden. An interesting note is that during the policeless time of the war, we supposedly had the lowest crime rate ever.

Raids on homes and searches of houses were now rampant. Although no German ever entered our home, they quite often surrounded the house, and we could see them peering from behind trees with machine guns. I remember sitting in the baker's on the corner waiting to head off our police friends coming home from town and warn them of our unwelcome visitors.

Due to the curfews, my mother would sometimes stay in town after a dinner party. Besides the police in residence, we had transient "guests" all the time. At times the phone would go at night with warnings to whoever were staying there to make themselves scarce. I remember answering a few of these phone calls, awakening our boarders to hurry them out and, with the nanny and the maid, busying myself with the burning of damaging legal papers in the old iron kitchen stove. Next to it stood what we called the hay box. Into its cozy sawdust-filled interior we always put boiling pots to keep them simmering and thus save on gas. Underneath the pots and sawdust I'd hide the papers to be kept, figuring there was no German patriotic enough to burn his fingers.

I had my own secret hiding place under a loose flagstone on the terrace. Here I kept my diary, an American flag which had been given to me by a cousin the night he fled to Sweden, special editions of the underground news, an early picture of Churchill and the usual paraphernalia a child wants to keep from the grown-ups. On these nights, this flagstone was double-checked by flashlight.

That last war winter, the Germans started taking over hotels and schools and any other space they could find to house the ever-swelling stream of German refugees pouring into Denmark as the allies gained ground on the Eastern and Western fronts. By the end of the war, we had nearly a million of them, mainly old men, women and children who lived in abject conditions, barely looked after by their own. We would see horse-drawn carts going through town piled with blanket-covered bodies, off to be cremated at some unknown destination. Our school didn't escape, either, and we were moved into an adjacent teacher training college to continue classes in afternoon sessions. We still shared the same playground except for a huge fence going through the middle—a mini Berlin wall. From our class windows, we could watch a motley crew of Hitler *jugend,* no more than twelve years old, practicing their military drill work, and thin old men and women in ragged clothes with small children on their laps sitting around the wall watching with sad white faces.

The last two months of the war, much to our joy, we stayed home from school altogether. With five other girls, I had a private tutor—a rather dashing young teacher who in no way knew how to cope with us. He could be seen running down the road waving ruler and book, trying to call us all back to class. But we had other ideas, and at this point our parents had greater worries than our scholastic attainments.

Almost every commodity was nearly impossible to get. My feet, like the rest of me, were growing alarmingly fast. The pair of shoes one was allotted a year had to be bought with considerable foresight. Hence, the safe choice of size 9, although I never grew beyond size 7 and had to stuff enormous wads of cotton into the toes. They would stay on, but gave one a rather slow, ducklike gait, rather limiting one's activities. Perhaps Mother knew what she was doing after all.

My mother's clothes were passed on to me and with a bit of lengthening and letting out managed to fit. My clothes were passed on to my sister, which was all right, for at least it got me out of the hated smock dresses and matching pants which were much beneath my dignity at age thirteen. New raincoats were made out of old bed sheets sent to the cleaner's to be impregnated with water-repellents, then fashioned into rather smart trench coats. Anything was usable: old curtains, plaid tartans, rabbit skins and even flat fish skin fashioned into shoes, handbags and belts. Even dog wool was knit into mittens and gloves. The dogs were cold, but we were warm.

An event that made a deep impression on us children was when the English bombed the Gestapo headquarters in the Shell Building and, by mistake, also hit the French Catholic school. The raid took place in late morning, March 21, 1945, its prime object to destroy the Gestapo files. However, the Gestapo kept their Danish prisoners on the top floor. The carefully planned bombing was most successful—in a few moments, the entire building was in flames, but most of the prisoners were able to escape by jumping out and walking down through the rubble. The tragedy that occurred later was caused by the squadron's leader's plane crashing into the school. Possibly his fellow pilots thought it another military target and bombed it thoroughly. Sadly, rescuers were unable to reach those inside in time: eighty-six children and thirteen grown-ups perished. When Mother told us of the catastrophe, we identified strongly with the victimized children.

We all knew the end of the war was near.

Finally at six in the afternoon on May 4, 1945, the much-awaited announcement came. The Danish speaker we'd heard all through the war on the B.B.C. from London now read the moving news in a near sobbing voice. The Germans were surrendering unconditionally in Holland, northwest Germany and Denmark at eight the next morning. We waited a few seconds to hear the fate of Norway, but the sadness that they were not included could not really dampen our joy. We all kissed, embraced and cried, as millions did that evening. The flag was fetched and quickly raised. I rushed upstairs to get a huge piece of orange candy, which had been given to me on my birthday in 1941 and which I'd sworn then not to eat until the end of the war. It was a bit dusty but absolutely delicious. I ran to my secret flagstone and got my American flag, which I tied to my bicycle, and then raced off with all my friends.

45

Everybody's front door was wide open, the hated blackout curtains were being burned and bottles of Cherry Heering and carefully guarded wine were poured out to friends and strangers alike. The next two days were total chaos. We all went to town to welcome the English troops who arrived at the same time as the Free Danish Army coming from Sweden. Almost immediately afterward the Americans arrived too. We collected autographs from every Allied soldier we could get near and patiently stood outside the various garrisons they had taken over, ready with our basic school English: "Please, do you have some chewing gum?" We kids also raced up and down on our bicycles in front of the hotel and garrisons in our village where the Germans and their refugees still were housed, shouting and waving our flags at them and singing English songs.

There was sporadic shooting through the town as the Danes now started rounding up collaborators and this only added to the excitement. A few days after the surrender, we heard that a collaborator was besieged in a house near ours. The resistance people had surrounded the property and were exchanging volleys of shots with the fugitive. It was a miracle that no one was killed, considering the casual way everyone crowded to watch. Suddenly the shooting stopped and the house was rushed. The traitor had finally committed suicide. As the body was carried out, we children thronged about the stretcher and spat on it, the only tribute we considered fit for a traitor.

Liberation

The first few weeks of liberation were a perpetual celebration, and the atmosphere of joy
and jubilation pervaded everything. For a short time, we were
part of the adult world: bedtimes were forgotten, we drank
wine with the grown-ups, they ate lollypops with us, and all
thoughts of schedules and disciplines went happily out the
window. As in the war years, when everyone had been so
open and sharing of what little he had, so did this warmth
continue those first few months after the war.

Our home was full of English and American friends and
people from abroad whom we hadn't seen for years. Everyone
was eagerly questioned as to the fate of friends still missing.
What excitement to answer the doorbell and find a long-lost
friend, someone one hadn't seen for years and whose fate had
been unknown. The conversation was practically all in English, much to our frustration, but if you're curious enough—
and we were—it's a great way to pick up a language.

The conversation of course was mainly about war exploits.
I wish I could remember them all, or even tell them in the
chair-gripping fashion in which they were originally told. My
uncle, the one who had sent us the marvelous Christmas card,
also returned with some of his tales, one of them about the

time he was guarding Professor Nils Bohr, the physicist so important to the Allies in developing the atom bomb. Prof. Bohr had been transported to Sweden where, closely guarded, he had been installed in a flat. My uncle was part of the heavily armed bodyguard waiting impatiently to send him off to London in a Spitfire specially ordered for his transportation. Stockholm, being neutral during the war, was naturally a nest of international intrigue and spies. Therefore, his presence had to be totally secret and anonymous. Finally came the night he was to be shipped off to England and everyone could relax. He was dutifully delivered into the hands of the English pilot at the airport and, upon the bodyguard's return to the flat, the celebration of relief started with much booze and noisy revelry. At 3:00 A.M., the doorbell rang. Instant silence and sobriety. Who on earth could *that* be? Outside the door stood Prof. Bohr, all by himself. As a change in the weather had not permitted takeoff, he had calmly bid the pilot farewell and taken a taxi back home, no guard or anything. Sheepishly, everyone resumed his vigil, and a few days later he left.

It was in these stories that the humor rather than the tragedy of the war was recalled.

Many were the tales of Danish fishermen ferrying refugees to Sweden in the dark of the night. The one problem prevalent during these secret transfers seemed to have been the nonswimmers. More than a few times when a German patrol boat approached, the fishing captain would pass the word to his "cargo": "Jump overboard and swim!" Back came the answer: "I can't!"

I remember my uncle's showing us Himmler's black eye patch, a souvenir he'd been given by the English Intelligence, with whom he'd ferreted out the S.S. Chief's last hiding place. Just before and all during the war, my uncle had been in and out of Germany many times, smuggled in Danish herring trucks, but we knew nothing of this until after liberation. His pursuit of Martin Bormann after the war lasted for years, but those tales are still locked in the Archives.

Into the midst of all the festivities arrived Annelise, floor-length gray pleated uniform, starched apron, peaked cap, badge and all. My thirteen years and five-foot-seven curtsied nicely to her eighteen and five-feet-four. Annelise Rubenstein and her brother had fled to Sweden in October, 1943, with many other Danish Jews. Her route to safety had been through a small church in northern Zealand, where she had been hidden by the parson in the choir loft for days before being put on a fishing boat to freedom. After two years of training in a Swedish home for children, she returned to Denmark right after liberation and became our governess. Annelise became more of a friend than a governess as she was practically my contemporary, but she still had the difficult task of being a figure of authority. Postscript: She kept in contact with the parson and his family and, when he was prematurely widowed, eventually married him. They now have a family and a new parish of their own.

The Jews had not been victims of instant persecution in Denmark. The order to round them up finally came in October, 1943, at Rosh Hashanah. Three days before, the German naval attaché leaked the grim news to two Danish friends active in the underground, which immediately sprang into action. Because of the warning, nearly seven thousand Danish Jews were able to escape to Sweden. Of the five hundred Jews captured and taken to Teresienstadt, considered one of the "milder" German concentration camps, fifty died. These were the weak and elderly, deprived of the medicines packed in the regular shipments of Danish Red Cross packages. Both the underground members later served as Socialist-Democrat prime ministers: Hans Hedtoft and H.C. Hansen. The naval attaché, G. F. Duckwitz, not only was decorated by the Danish government after the war, but eventually returned to Copenhagen as the West German ambassador.

That summer the documentary films taken in Auschwitz, Belsen and Dachau were shown in the Danish cinemas, so we all saw them.

Amidst the postwar swarm of uniforms, I was immensely pleased to put on my own. I had, in the last year of the war, become the youngest member of the junior corps of *Danske Kvinders Beredskab,* a civil defense women's auxiliary. Our group of eight to ten girls had been taught general first aid, how to put out fire bombs, field maneuvers to identify military vehicles and planes, and map and terrain reading. At the close of the war, we still had field training but also turned our attention to more humane works, like finding and distributing clothing and food to refugees. We stayed in a Boy Scout camp for terrain training and every morning took our constitutional trailing after a handsome, smartly dressed lieutenant complete with swagger stick. Up hill and down dale we went—in hot pursuit of *him,* but he didn't know it.

Autumn saw us back in our own school again. That first morning assembly, when we walked into a building renovated, repaired and repainted after the refugees had left, was as moving to pupils as to teachers. I don't think there has ever been a group of children so happy to return to school as we were that particular morning.

The country was slowly returning to normal, though the shortages would remain for a long while. We were taken on excursions to Sweden across Øre Sound. Sweden, whose bright lights could always be seen from blacked-out Denmark all through the war, was to us like the vision of the little match girl of Hans Christian Andersen. The ferry took about two hours, and it was like arriving in fairyland. Hot chocolate, huge cream cakes, oranges and bananas and real elastic to put into your knickers! My very first nanny had been Swedish and had kept in touch with us before and after the war. Now we went to visit her. She used to send packages to us all the time, filled with the things we still couldn't get, a really lovely thing to do.

The first thing I got in Sweden was a bright yellow corduroy skirt—I'd never seen corduroy before—with a white deer and flower-printed blouse to match. The first time I wore it, we went for Easter lunch at my uncle's. Afterward, we all went out and sat in the early spring sun watching the pool being filled. As the water reached the top, two of my cousins pushed me in, new clothes and all. Remembering the synthetic war-time materials, which would shrink in all directions at first contact with water, I knew I would emerge from the pool in "two sizes too small." Never before or since have I felt such hate as I did for my cousins when I hit the water—never mind the water's being 45°. I spent the rest of the afternoon in abject misery until the outfit was dried out—and I discovered it hadn't shrunk at all.

The yellow outfit was part of my confirmation wardrobe. Overnight, having been confirmed in the Lutheran Church, I was considered a young lady, whatever that meant. The Lutheran confirmation, as I look back upon it, seems more like a commercial exploitation than a landmark of spiritual attainment. To justify this statement, I'll have to explain a few things about it. You are initially baptized into the Lutheran faith, this faith to be confirmed at age fourteen, a totally confusing time anyway. Before this event, you spend a half year going to your parish parson for instructions, Bible readings and interpretation of same. There's no doubt about your faith, but relating it to everyday life is a different matter in early adolescence. One experienced the emotional fervor of a novice all according to the parson's eloquence and dramatic sense, and one faithfully kept on saying *his* evening prayers.

I remember so clearly the speculations everybody in our class (and for that matter, our other contemporaries) had as to what the "harvest" would be. Girls were given long white dresses to be worn to church, or the boys their first dark suits. One's entire wardrobe was changed from child's to adult's— in those days, there was no such acknowledged thing as the separate world of the teen. One received fountain pens, cigarette cases, radios, monogrammed luggage, cameras if they were available, even a new bed and pillow in my case, jewelry and engraved compacts—all the worldly trappings of adult life. The curious thing, however, was that similar festivities were arranged by the town officials for the agnostics.

In the concert hall, speeches proclaimed *their* stepping into the world of the grown-ups amid the same shower of presents and parties. At the time, I discussed with my oldest friend, Marita, all aspects of this "something-for-everyone" celebration, and there must have been something that grated for us to discuss it at all. But then, again, it *was* tradition. . . .

51

Being "grown-up," though still fourteen and very young, meant balls and weekend parties in the summer. The transition to ball gowns and long white gloves from shapeless and clumsy school outfits was quite something. These rigs consisted of layer upon layer of woolies, woolens and wool. For starters, we wore long undervests with clip-on elastics, which hooked on to the familiar scratchy stocking, invariably bagging around the ankles by mid-morning. The only advantage the undervest had was that by hooking it very tightly to the stocking, one could flatten the embarrassing bulge of budding breasts. Then, there were under-knickers and the most detested over-knickers. Whenever my mother met me after school for cakes and tea, just to make sure I hadn't pulled the over-knickers above my knees, she'd lift my skirt right in the middle of the restaurant to check—I was thirteen at the time! *That* was the ultimate humiliation! It also annoyed me immensely when, after I'd fought a long uphill battle for my first pair of silk stockings or some other grown-up apparel, Sussi was granted the same permission shortly afterward. But, I guess that is the lot of the firstborn.

The winters were long and dark with an hour's bicycling to the station and another hour on the train to school, reversing the process in the afternoon. Daylight, let alone sun, is very scarce or practically nonexistent mid-winter in Denmark. In fact, we're not unlike the Finns who allegedly say, "We fish, we drink and make love during summer; during winter, we don't fish." This, of course, didn't fully apply to us kids. There was little if any time to do much else besides homework.

The Sunday before confirmation our dolls had been solemnly wrapped in newspaper and packed away after a last game of "Emergency Ward." Our eyes had already started roving, and the train to and from school was the perfect place for field studies of the opposite sex. We were oblivious to the smell of wet woolen garments in steamy train compartments, while we secretly developed crushes on our fellow commuters. They were recognized and labeled by their overcoats, and the daydreaming adventures we had with those "overcoats" might have set even Freud to speculating. After vacations, one did the distance to the station in half-time to find if one's favorite "green tweed" was still on the 7:09.

But, the facts of life were still a complete mystery to me. One never talked to one's mother about anything like *that*. My first indication of womanhood sent me scurrying to the attic where I hid sobbing my heart out for half a day thinking I had some horrible fatal disease. I really thought I was dying.

The summer of '46 saw invitations to the formal country balls arriving by the dozen. They were beautifully engraved, often with family crest, and two balls at neighboring homes meant spending the entire weekend. I'd pack up my two ball gowns, two pairs of long white gloves, my only pair of white size 9 shoes and join one of the groups going by train or car. These same shoes and gloves could present certain embarrassing problems. The gloves, which had belonged to our mothers and grandmothers, were always drenched in talc and packed away between parties. Despite the vigorous shaking the gloves received before each wearing, there were always traces of the powder, and frequently one's dancing partners ended up with big white handprints on the back of their formal black jackets. Some hostesses, to liven things up, would suddenly clap their hands and ask each girl to place an object, usually her right shoe, into a large sack, to be claimed by an unknown partner. Mortified, we would have to admit ownership of Grandmother's twelve-year-old silver sandals or the size 9's with the cotton wool lumps in the toes. The dances were chaperoned by the elders, who would sit along the edge of the dance floor carefully watching us. Behind their backs we would call this long row of gaping authority "The Meat Loaf."

Being one of the youngest and very shy, I used to dread these weekends and dances and would do anything to get out of them, although sometimes I had to admit I did have fun. The guests were divided between the two homes or sometimes put up at the local inn, but always carefully segregated. During the days, we'd swim, play croquet or tennis or to go picnics, catching up on gossip since last we'd met. And then, in the evening, the dancing began. It was quite a lovely sight —all the girls in long flowing dresses, the boys in black tie or the occasional dress uniform of young aspiring officers—especially as we moved through "The Lancers." These were sets of intricate group dances with prearranged patterns and steps that everyone had learned years before at the then-hateful ballroom dancing classes of Mr. Hans Beck. I suppose they were a cross-blend of the formality of court dances, of square dancing and the Scottish reel, and terribly rough on ballgown hems if one had a partner with too-large feet. There were other types of dances, of course, and frequent trips to punch bowl or bar, depending upon the host's open-mindedness. The ultimate of daring was hand-holding walks in the dark and a fleeting kiss behind a bush.

At one such weekend ball—I was seventeen by then—the host was decidedly close-minded: no liquor whatsoever. Some of the young men were nearly twenty-one and highly indignant at this slap at their manhood, muttering under their breaths that they were "old enough to fight for King and country but not old enough to have a drink in this place."

Finally two Norwegian boys (with the social status of "ball cavaliers") decided to take some action. Grabbing another girl and myself, they found their car and we drove into the village to the local pub. Sometime later we drove back onto the castle grounds straight into complete pandemonium: full orchestra blaring from the central courtyard, gamekeeper running through the woods tooting a huge waldhorn and host and chaperones in a state of hand-wringing consternation. Apparently, half the party had disappeared—the four of us to the pub and several other couples ostensibly to explore the surrounding woods—and our host was determined to round up all the strays as fast as possible. When the head count was once again correct, the drawbridge was raised—and no more hanky-panky in the woods.

For me there weren't any heavy or enduring relationships, at least at that time. Very few of us went steady, for instance, which I think was more fun, although one moved from ball to ball with the same group of people.

But the event most important to Sussi and me that year we weren't allowed to attend: Mother and Uncle Hugo slipped off quietly one September day in 1946 and were married. Sussi's and my long-discussed plans to be bridesmaids had been completely foiled.

The marriage entailed moving house, and that prospect was not so attractive—I had to leave the home I'd grown up in. Two days were spent dejectedly walking around the garden taking leave of favorite flowers and trees, finally moping to the attic where I crawled up on the top shelf with all the suitcases and bawled my eyes out for a couple of hours—then I was ready to leave.

Uncle Hugo's family fortune had been made in textiles, and they owned factories and plants throughout Denmark, Norway and Sweden. Ironically, I'd spent many summer weeks at Uncle Hugo's house as a child. His former wife was a patron of the ballet and each summer had invited some of the children from the Royal Ballet School to stay at the house and put on performances and recitals. I'd studied ballet for six years from the time we'd returned from Rapallo, but by age twelve, I was already five-foot-seven and saw no future in being the biggest swan in the back row, so I'd quit. Nevertheless, I loved to take part in the summer dancing in my own unprofessional way and often shared a room there with Toni Lander, who has since become a prima ballerina of both the Danish National and New York City Ballet companies. When we moved, I was allowed to have the same tower room I'd always had as a guest in Uncle Hugo's house.

"Piniehøj" was situated by the sea halfway between Copenhagen and Elsinore. It was a huge house, in retrospect not a complete architectural success, but very spacious and, in Mother's impeccable taste, beautifully decorated with antiques. We had our own beach, tennis court, hothouses and various "lust-houses," the literal Danish translation of the always-empty Victorian garden pavilions. On the grounds were three landmark Viking graves, one of which had been excavated by the government (the other two cannot be touched until the year 2000). The main house was built in 1901 by an architect who was building Parliament at the same time and, therefore, had little time to dabble with our beach cottage. He must have had some leftover gargoyles, for there were several spouting rain-water from the roof gutters to the gardens below. What's more, he forgot the kitchen—he literally forgot it! This was really a blessing as it turned out, for half the cavernous base-ment became the cook's domain. There was also a guest villa, and a large carriage house with staff quarters and the gar-dener's flat above. Across the road were our vegetable and fruit gardens, with chicken coops, dove cotes and the stables alongside. There were always bowlsful of huge, juicy straw-berries and raspberries set out in the kitchen for evening snacks, and I don't think I've tasted any so delicious since.

Of all the beautiful aspects of that house, the sea was an incomparable joy to me. How many times I walked the beach: at dawn when the stars were still out and the sunrise just a hint of pink over the horizon; at midday, with the bright sun re-flecting on the waves as though they were part of an immense prism; in late afternoon, when the water turned a leaden blue-black and the winds peculiar to a storm sent the seagulls screeching for shelter; late at night, when the moon seemed to have a calming effect on the water, and the lapping of the waves lulled me to sleep. No matter the time of day or the season, I always found great strength and respite from the problems of my world on the shore of the sea. To this day, I'm never very happy to be too far from the ocean for long, and getting back always seems to restore my spirit.

As before when I had hidden in the garden or woods around "Bernstorffslund" after being scolded or reprimanded or just to be alone, I now vanished down the beach. Some-times I'd fall asleep, sending my mother into a state of agita-tion and the entire household out to find me. *That* was no small production: the chauffeur led, followed by the two maids, the cook, the scullery maid, the three gardeners, and Annelise closing the ranks, plus whoever else might be visiting us at the time. I could never understand, after I returned bleary-eyed and with sand in my hair, what all the fuss had been about—*I* knew where I was.

Discipline was strict in certain things. Five minutes to six, we met at the grandfather's clock; one minute to six, we were behind the chairs at the dinner table; one minute past six, if we were *not* there, meant dinner in the kitchen. Punctuality was the one thing Uncle Hugo insisted upon, to the point that we always had to arrive for everything five minutes ahead of time, even if it meant waiting outside a host's front door in the snow or rain until the appointed hour. He always used to say, "People's time is the only thing you have no right to waste because you can't make up for it." Being a bit absentminded, I exaggerated this rule on several occasions, showing up for parties one week and five minutes ahead of schedule. There was nothing more embarrassing than sitting perched on the edge of a chair in my best evening dress, waiting for the chauffeur to pick me up and watching the host family eating their meatballs and mashed potatoes while trying to make polite conversation.

Uncle Hugo never interfered with Mother's raising us. On the contrary, he spoiled us, often slipping each of us ten or fifteen krones to go to the cinema, in those days an outrageous sum which my mother pretended not to see.

When I wasn't at the movies, which was most of my free time, I was singing hymns and Gregorian chants with the "Angel Choir." The "angels" were a group of friends who'd gotten together merely to share their joy of singing. Sad to say, our only public performance was at the Dutch ambassador's funeral.

Uncle Hugo loved fishing, and during the tuna season in Øresund, I'd go out with him often. He told me of the time my father had spent thirty-six hours bringing in a giant tuna and how it had dragged him from the north of Zealand to the top of Jutland twice. The fishermen were sure if it hadn't been for the tuna's loss of blood in the struggle, it would have set a world record in size and weight. On that trip, my father had taken along two guests whom he didn't know very well. They later reported him for cruelty to animals. Meanwhile, my father was being spoon-fed by my mother, since he was unable to use his arms for a week.

One summer we went to Laederlen in Norway for a week, but that was less amusing. My stepfather and his friends had for years rented the fishing rights to part of the river, but women were not allowed to fish there (Women's Lib would have taken kindly to *this* rule!). It took my mother a week of fishless frustration to discover they'd given her a hookless fly as a joke. For us there was nothing to do but climb mountains —a wet amusement as it rained constantly—or read, or eat salmon for breakfast, lunch and dinner. How little one knew of gourmet delicacies then.

Late that summer back at Piniehøj, we had a visit from the family's most distinguished member: Sigrid Undset, my grandmother's sister. She'd won the Nobel Prize for Literature in 1928 for her trilogy, *Kristin Lavransdatter,* and was probably the best-known Norwegian of her time. Her painter-husband and their daughter had died before the war, and their older son was killed fighting the Germans. She and the younger son had fled Norway through Russia to America at the time of the invasion. In America she had lectured and helped raise funds for the unbearably hard-pressed Norwegians (I recall during the war all Danish children being asked to contribute weekly from their pocket money to help serve a daily meal of milk and porridge to every Norwegian child).

My sister and I were overwhelmed by this stately, formidable presence and stared at her silently. Then in her late sixties, she was a tall, gray-haired lady of heroic proportions, wearing a long black dress and a serious but serene expression on her face. She left late that afternoon, and we never saw her again. When she died in 1949, she was given a state funeral. My mother attended and described for us the impressive assemblage of royalty, state dignitaries, clergy and a special emissary from the Vatican (Sigrid had long before converted to the Catholic faith).

The funeral was at Lillehammer, in a small country cemetery atop a hill. While the priests were solemnly conducting the service, a small boy carrying a fishing rod with a live trout still on the hook suddenly appeared over the crest of the hill. His mouth fell open, his blue eyes became saucers, as he gaped at this mass of silken robes, dress uniforms with medals, sashes and plumes, and great clouds of incense wafting over all. He stood stock still taking it all in, then fled in a twink, leaving only the trout flopping in the grass.

Some twelve years ago when there was talk in Denmark of making a film of *Kristin Lavransdatter,* my name was brought forward. Frederik and I were established performers by then and had done two or three movies in Europe. However, I had not had the dramatic acting experience necessary to tackle such a role and was far too young for the part anyway, so the notion was quickly abandoned, and the movie eventually shelved.

Late in 1948 my stepfather suffered a stroke, which required his getting away for a long rest. His doctor recommended a sea voyage. As there were still restrictions on buying foreign currency and very few liners operating, my parents chose a Norwegian freighter. Mother got into quite a hassle with our headmistress, who strenuously objected to our missing months of school. However, my mother prevailed, as usual, pointing out the trip would be educational and "Who knows if they'll ever get the chance again?" We left that December on the *Cometa* bound for South America.

The first few days out of Aarhus were a bit tense as we steered very cautiously through the remains of German mine fields in a pea-soup fog. It was the captain's last voyage before retirement, and I think he was exacting his revenge for all the hundreds of idiotic, boring questions he'd had to answer over the years by booming out grim, pessimistic forecasts of our chances of surviving. He continued this gloom right through the Bay of Biscay, where we met three days of the worst storm that had been seen for years. I was so seasick through all of it, I prayed for a mine to end my misery.

We were five of the twelve passengers. The other seven included three Norwegians who had been German sympathizers, one a woman en route to Argentina to join her husband who'd escaped arrest. Sussi and I played with her small son, but otherwise they were totally ostracized. As we neared the Equator and calmer waters, I would sit in the bow every night and watch the dancing phosphorescence or visit the "spark," the wireless operator, here as often on Scandinavian ships a woman. This, I decided, would be my calling in life!

I also struck up a close friendship with the cook. Before we'd left, I'd had two impacted wisdom teeth removed and now, halfway across the Atlantic, developed a massive infection. With no doctor aboard, the cook made a thick poultice of boiling oatmeal porridge to hold to my cheek. The agony was immense, but then so was the fear of the vintage hypodermic and penicillin, which no one knew how to use. The "home cure" worked—just in time for me to be duly dunked and christened as we crossed the Equator. In gratitude, I became his galley slave for life.

After two weeks at sea, we sailed into Rio harbor in an early morning mist. To describe all the impressions and dramatic impact on me would be impossible, it being my first trip to a really different part of the world, and one of the most exotic at that. It's the funny little vignettes one remembers most, and one of them was when we went to Corcovado to admire the immense statue of Jesus Christ, as much a landmark as Sugartop. After a long trip through fog and jungle, we finally stood in front of the statue, awed by its majesty. As we were buying postcards and watermelon from the little carts nearby, it started to pour as only it can do in the tropics. Suddenly a little door opened in the base of the statue, and into the dry safety of Jesus's feet rolled watermelons, postcards, vendors and all.

On to Santos, where I found a surprise gift from the cook of an entire stalk of half-ripe bananas hung over my bunk. I'd never seen a whole stalk before, and it very nearly finished me off. Twenty-four bananas and one violent stomach ache later, we sailed into Buenos Aires. There on the dock was a large reception committee of German- and Norwegian-speaking people, complete with flags, songs and all. It was obviously not for us, but for the Norwegian outcasts, and the rest of us on board were shocked.

It was Christmas Eve, which we'd anticipated spending with some old family friends, the van Pallandts, Baron van Pallandt being the Dutch ambassador to Argentina and Uruguay. We'd not seen them since before the war, and Mother had decided to turn up on their doorstep and surprise them. (Social note: You should never go halfway around the world to surprise your friends without knowing if they're really there.) Quite right. The Embassy was locked and shuttered, and we spent Christmas Eve in the Norwegian Seamen's Mission. The temperature was almost 104°F., and the humidity unbearable. With no air conditioning, we just sat there and sweated. Halfway through our dripping feeble attempt at Christmas hymns, the second officer got so drunk he threw the Christmas tree out into the street, candles and all. Nobody objected—it was too hot.

We later learned the van Pallandts had left Buenos Aires for their summer (Christmas) holidays some days before and had been in Montevideo all the time we'd been there. The ship was drydocked for two weeks for repairs, having been damaged going through the locks into Buenos Aires, so we moved into a hotel. As I recall, it was called the Plaza, but since there's a "Plaza" in every town, that's a safe guess. At any rate, it was most elegant, with air conditioning, thick carpets, endless corridors and luxurious rooms—and I got fleas! A day after checking in, I was covered with welts. Mother, convinced the sheets had not been changed and the hotel was at fault, cornered the maid who summoned the housekeeper who summoned the director. Under great protest in front of this committee, I was made to pull up my skirt, pull down my panties and stand there, mortified, while they examined my derriere—"Exhibit A"—and argued over the origins of my discomfort. I got my own back when Mother returned from a shopping spree and indignantly told me she'd been pinched at least five times. To this day, I think her vanity secretly enjoyed this boost.

We returned to Montevideo, and finally caught up with the Pallandt family. Baroness Elsa van Pallandt, Danish-born, had been a childhood friend of my mother's and her family had long owned *Berlingske Tidende,* the paper my father had directed. Their daughter, Clara, who was Sussi's age, later spent several school semesters and summer holidays with us while the family was posted to Stalinist Russia, and their son, Frederik, also spent college vacations with us.

61

We went to the house in Carasco, a resort area outside Montevideo, and Frederik opened the door, the first time we'd met since babyhood. We've been opening all kinds of "doors" for each other ever since, always having the same odd sensation we felt that first time, literally recognizing and instantly loving a kindred soul.

He was tall—six-foot-four even then—slender and blonde with smoky blue eyes. He was fifteen, I sixteen. I was determined not to be escorted by my mother's preselected five-foot-two Uruguayan gentleman when we went to the Casino that evening. Frederik and I willfully maneuvered it in such a way that we spent the entire evening together and next to each other. During dinner, the croupier suddenly turned up. Uncle Hugo had gambled earlier in the evening, leaving some chips which he'd believed to be 10's instead of 100's, and his numbers had come in consistently ever since. Out of this windfall, he paid for all twenty-four guests, gave my mother and Aunt Else money for a visit to Dior the next day and, when we finally left, having danced till 1:00 A.M., bought the whole basket of gardenias a little old lady was selling outside.

The next day the two families went to the beach, and Frederik plunged into the icy sea with me on his heels. Both sets of parents watched in complete amazement, knowing full well their respective offspring could not normally be dragged into that frigid water under any circumstances.

After much too short a visit, we had to say goodbye. Before leaving I smuggled a carton of cigarettes to Frederik from the freighter. I'd already started smoking. "If you want to ruin your health, I'm not going to bribe you to refrain from your stupidity," my mother had stated. Cigarettes were scarce in Denmark for years after the war, and my cousins and I used to roll our own. The tobacco came from my stepfather's partially smoked butts. Years before, he'd gone to Egypt to cure his tuberculosis of the knee: the best remedy then was being buried in the hot sands twice daily, which he faithfully did. (He also kept his twelve-meter yacht on the Nile, taking his private physician for sails each evening. I wonder how one would file a Blue Cross claim for *that!*) He'd learned to smoke only two puffs of the Egyptian cigarettes before snuffing them out, and it was this unused tobacco that we spirited off to the kitchen stairs. For papers, we turned to an antique Bible my cousin had found in the library, and if Mother had ever checked, she would have found half of St. Luke missing—he'd gone up in smoke. Those cigarettes always gave me a bad conscience, but I wanted to be part of the gang.

When we'd returned to Copenhagen, I had to work furiously to catch up with my studies and also decide what to do when I finished high school. Except for the advent of summer and Mother's immense hospitality filling Piniehøj with friends, friends' friends, and friends' friends' friends, the next year-and-a-half was spent studying. At the end of my senior year, there would be one comprehensive exam covering three years of work, and my success in it would determine my future plans. Having a great facility for languages, I'd already decided to continue at University to become a translator or teacher but I definitely wanted first a year or two abroad. In Mother's mind there was no doubt I would go to Cambridge or Oxford—that was the "done" thing. However, I had other ideas. When I suggested going to America, Mother protested, "But, they don't speak English!" And a dinner guest added, "Scratch them and you'll still find feathers!"

My bosom pal, next-door neighbor in school and comrade-in-arms during the war, was the daughter of a prominent jurist who was also a special adviser to the American Embassy. Into Birgit ("Bee") Carstensen's home came various prominent American visitors plus lots of American students.

I'd often joined her and her family at the giant outdoor Fourth of July celebration in Rebild Hills. One year at the special dinner afterward, the more than eight hundred invited guests suffered food poisoning. We'd arrived halfway through the main course, missing the tainted pâté and tongue, only to discover in the ladies' room dozens of victims perched over the loos and sinks throwing up. Behind every pillar and tree in the parks and gardens there was someone heaving. Within minutes, all the neighboring fire brigades and police vehicles were carting off green-faced

63

guests to end their celebrating in the hospital wards. So much for Danish-American relations!

Through Bee, I heard of the American-Danish foundation and we both applied for scholarships. These were awarded on grades and an essay on why we wanted to go to America. I can't remember what I wrote, but I must have said the right things. We had a first, second and third choice of colleges, and my first was the University of Southern California—only because of climate, and not due to any knowledge whatsoever of its academic standards.

Bee and I slaved through exams and finally won our white graduation caps. By tradition, graduating students in Denmark have free license to carry on alarmingly for a week after exams. Our class of fourteen, the smallest Zahles School had known in a long time, lacked nothing in spirit riding through town in open horse-drawn trolleys (charabancs), dancing around the horse statue in one of the main squares (a tradition) and singing academic and drinking songs. With the help of the neighboring boys' schools and various beaux, we painted the town red.

Capping all this graduation happiness were our acceptance letters, mine from U.S.C., Bee's from Bryn Mawr. I presented Mother with the letter and, to my surprise, she was pleased and very proud. Typically, she immediately plunged into preparations for my departure.

As she put me on the plane for Los Angeles late that summer, her last words to me were, "Well, at least I suppose you'll learn to speak American."

Star-Spangled
and Striped

I left for Los Angeles that summer of 1951
with visions of sunshine and blue seas and
gleaming beaches, after having spent nineteen years of my life
in half-years of semi-darkness, winter and snow. When I arrived in my mother's tailored suit, hat, gloves, high-heeled
shoes and earrings, clutching her large handbag, I quickly
realized looking at the strolling groups of students in saddle
shoes, ponytails and blue jeans, that I was "the vision." But,
everyone was very polite about it and they all managed to
keep a straight face. If anyone saw anything odd about me, the
giggles were saved until I wasn't listening. Actually, since I
was the first Danish student the University of Southern California had ever had, perhaps they wrote the whole thing off
as some version of eccentric native dress. The university paper
ran my picture with an informative little caption about "Nina
Moller" without the umlaut, which always sounded like some
sort of tooth disease to me. Within two days everybody hailed
me on the campus by first name and I was grateful for this
friendly manner. I was asked many peculiar questions like: "Is
it true there are ice bears walking in the streets of Copenhagen?" or, "Are you still occupied by the Germans?" This time
it was my turn to keep a straight face.

My major was to be in languages and education if ever I got through the insane ritual known as registration—the queuing was agony in high heels. With a lot of help from my curious but friendly classmates my schedule finally became a reality. Because of Denmark's higher standard of secondary education I was enrolled as a sophomore. My living quarters that first year were in an off-campus cooperative, a rambling old clapboard house with porch and palm trees and some twenty-odd girls from all over the world. Because the arrangements entailed our taking turns with the cooking and cleaning, I had brought with me all sorts of Danish cookbooks. This was something quite new to me as I had never done more than make a cup of tea, but with a lot of help from the books I muddled through and not badly at that. I must add that cooking has since become one of my favorite occupations: the bigger the dinner and more complicated the dish, the better.

My first roommate was an English girl who, within minutes of our meeting, decided my soul needed saving. This led to night-long philosophical and religious discussions, but she wasn't having much success. She dragged me off to several church-sponsored social functions, the first a bus trip to Palm Springs with much hymn singing, reciting of prayers and, as the high point of the weekend's festivities, roller skating in the basement of a church. That was okay with me, except that the glamorous movie star environment of Palm Springs I had read about didn't quite match these particular surroundings. Another trip took us to Death Valley which was much more interesting and beautiful. Later I met the pastor of my roommate's Presbyterian church. He looked like Gregory Peck, only more so, and her fervor became quite understandable. Having been allowed to take only two hundred dollars a year out of the country from the Danish National Bank to cover all my personal expenses (there were still very tight restrictions on buying foreign currency, though my mother occasionally managed little deals with friends from abroad), I decided to get a part-time job. The only thing available with my qualifications and permitted on my student visa was as a file clerk in the Veterans' Affairs office, a job with so little challenge that

66

I performed it in a near-zombie state. But at twenty-five cents per hour, who was I to complain?

Many of my evenings were spent boning up on Denmark's social and political structure, as I had been forewarned in the special orientation for foreign students that any one of us might be requested to speak before local groups. At last my moment came, when an Israeli housemate and I were asked to speak at a women's club in Los Angeles. We had been told by the dean of foreign students that the groups might offer us money and that, as impoverished foreign students, we should feel free to accept it, since guest speakers were often paid at such affairs. That really was welcome news.

Most of the night before the great event was spent writing what I considered a brilliant dissertation on the Danish social system. The next evening the club's hospitality chairman, a veritable living fat flower garden in an outrageous print dress with an orchid bobbing on her bosom, arrived to take us to the meeting. After a nervous sweaty-palmed drive, we arrived to find a hall full of gushing loud-speaking ladies, all with orchid-bedecked bosoms, scurrying about. We settled down and waited for the business of the evening to begin. The main discussion was whether or not the club would devote itself to crocheting booties for some baby home and, if so, was the color to be pink or blue and in what sizes and quantities. After hours of debate one wouldn't think possible, a vote was taken, the results of which I regret to say have slipped my mind. At 11:30 P.M. my friend and I were introduced. She made her speech about Israel and I followed with my incisive analysis of modern-day Denmark, to the polite applause, between yawns, of rows of glassy-eyed ladies with wilted corsages. We were told that we must, by all means, join them for refreshments. This turned out to be pumpkin pie, toward which I developed an instant hate. To me, it's the kind of food where every spoonful seems to grow larger and larger in your mouth and just stays there. Nevertheless, having been indoctrinated since childhood about the "starving Armenians," I dutifully ate all of the smallest piece possible.

Refreshments over, we were ceremoniously handed our

67

envelopes. I delightedly stuffed mine into my handbag, wanting to savor every moment of anticipation until I got back to my own room. Finally home, I flopped on the bed and tore open the envelope, relieved that there would be at least *something* to show for this never-ending evening. Out tumbled a check and I read the figure three times before it really registered. I held the thing, not knowing whether to curse or laugh. My payment, by signed and countersigned check, was one dollar! I never cashed it, hoping this would foul up their bank account but good in retaliation for what I considered a gross insult.

The atmosphere in the classrooms was relaxed and informal and so different from Europe. In Europe the professors lectured, their students slavishly took notes and sooner or later stood for a degree. Here the professors and students often got into rows and debates about what this philosopher or that writer really had in mind, but I was much too fearful in the beginning to take part in any of this. I also marveled at finding such courses as modern dance, theatre and other courses unheard of in European universities, and popped them into my schedule for as many credits as, say, a course in French. But I found the frequent exams or quizzes with their little "yes" or "no" answers kind of curious as I was used to long essays. I really loved the energy, optimism and activity which pervaded student life, and the breezy humor and comfortable rapport between students and faculty.

My first impressions are best taken from a letter to my sister, which my mother has kept all these years. " . . . can you believe that California is more than nine times as large as Denmark and the university has between twelve and fifteen thousand students, blocks and blocks of buildings and lawns, the size of a provincial Danish town? I took a bus downtown. Los Angeles is enormous and sprawling—it seems to me to have no center and, as a city, no soul. There are beautiful residential areas but they seem to be held together by used-car lots, gas stations and supermarkets. The supermarkets are unbelievable. Take anything, cut it up in slices, wrap it in plastic and that's a supermarket for you—I haven't seen a whole fish for sale yet! Here you also see an extraordinary sight—house-wives shopping in huge curlers. Can you imagine that sight in Copenhagen? They would get arrested for indecent exposure or offending public aesthetics. Everybody owns a car, even the students. That really makes me laugh when I think of all the dates I've driven home in Copenhagen because so few of them had cars—do you remember? Here you can't even share the expenses if you go out. The boys get most offended, and they are so much more polite."

To best describe the social scene—and with fifteen thousand students, that was quite a scene—I'll take some bits out of other letters. . . . "They've got this strange custom here—'necking,' they call it, i.e. kissing and pawing you when saying good night before you finally make a dash for the front door. It seems to be a rather meaningless ceremony in view of the fact that everybody does it with everybody. But, thank God, being a foreigner I am allowed my peculiarities and do not have to conform to every custom.

"I must tell you about one of the boys I have been out with —this will kill you. This very good-looking guy came up to me the other day when I was on my way to German class and invited me for dinner. He looked absolutely smashing in his ROTC uniform (it's too long to explain what *that* is), and I thought to myself, how lovely, how very nice. That evening we went out, and during dinner he proceeded to tell me that he had a free room in a mortuary, only he had to receive the "stiffs" that came in after midnight, a sort of nightclerk for unexpected guests. His description of the granny who died in her rocking chair and, when *rigor mortis* set in and she was still in this rocking chair position, and they had to pry her loose and couldn't straighten her out, really made me gag on my steak. I started smelling formaldehyde and all sorts of things. He was very nice, but there is just something about him that puts me off. To know that he is sleeping with all those stiffs down below! It really is a most extraordinary way of working your way through college."

I was also seeing a family friend, Hugo Wessel, who was enrolled at Occidental College. We had met at my home during summer holidays when I was sixteen, and I had developed an instant crush that grew into a summer romance kept alive by two years of correspondence. I even knitted him a pair of argyle socks which took two years to finish (and then I never could do the heels myself). He had also told me of U.S.C., not totally for unselfish reasons, perhaps. Hugo was handsome and dashing, and wheeling around in his Cadillac convertible was a rather marvelous way of seeing California.

Sometimes we would go to Santa Barbara, where he had relatives and friends. There I was introduced to the resident artists' colony in the foothills and took part in my first and only wine festival.

One Sunday we pulled up in front of one of their houses. It, like all the houses in the colony, was cozy inside but looked like a tossed salad of packing crates from the outside. One of the host's sons did scrap metal sculpture, and if I had to illustrate a moonscape, I'd photograph their front yard. An elderly white-haired bearded gentleman—our host—came out to shake hands and welcome us. He had the bluest eyes—and was stark naked. Never having encountered a naked host before, I summoned forth my mother's teaching of poise at all costs and at all times—and curtsied. He ushered us inside to a crowd of cheerful people, most of whom were artists and actors. There was a great deal of sampling of last year's vintage, then we went on to the more serious part of the procedures. Loads of grapes were dumped into a big vat out front. The custom was that the first grapes of the harvest had to be crushed by the feet of a virgin, and there was much ribald laughter as to who would qualify for that honor. Now, I looked about the youngest of the lot, let alone very virginal, and all eyes began turning toward me. For the first time my poise began waning. I nervously looked around but there was nobody near me. So without further ado, I lifted up my skirts and stepped into a foot or so of warm squishy grapes, quite like wading in jellyfish. Soon the other girls hopped in, too, and we tramped about in a circle stopping periodically for more samples of last year's vintage. I have one sharp recollection of an incredibly beautiful redhead dancing about with her skirt up to her waist and no knickers! As the afternoon wore on the laughter grew louder, the dancing wilder and someone started singing. The whole thing became a dizzy pleasant blur, and as the moon came up a bonfire was lit and everybody collapsed in a wine-sodden haze.

It was on the way back to U.S.C. from a beach party that Hugo and I smashed into a car that had crossed the center line into our lane. The driver was drunk but took off before the police arrived, and we never got his license number. Hugo's car was a mess, and my leg gashed badly. Nearby we found a sleepy old doctor who sewed me up and told me to take things easy for a while, but soon I undid all the good doctor's needlework. In an attempt at my usual routine of crossing from bathroom to bed in one giant leap, I executed the leap flawlessly, but the bed collapsed. My leg split open and we were off on a 4:00 A.M. visit to the downtown hospital emergency room—a side of L.A. and life I had not seen before.

The next day brought a bizarre phone call from a lawyer who introduced himself by saying he'd heard of my terrible accident (what terrible accident?). I must surely sue (sue whom?). I, of course, was suffering from discomfort and headaches (what headaches?). And what of my disability (so I couldn't play tennis or do the bunny-hop or whatever it was in those days)? We would, of course, split it down the middle, several thousand dollars, he said. Rubbish, I said, and hung up indignantly.

The next day I played tennis and split my leg for the third time, and that's enough of that! I still have two legs, albeit a bit darned.

My picture had run in the Los Angeles papers as a Danish curiosity, and as a result I was asked to appear on a TV quiz show called, "You Bet Your Life." Of course, I'd seen the Marx Brothers movies and loved Groucho, so I eagerly accepted. Although it appeared to the viewer that contestants were selected at random from the audience, we had all, in fact, been interviewed and screened in advance. We were then planted in the audience, and in my case, I had to wait till they asked for someone from a faraway place. While nervously waiting in my seat, I chatted with a young man who was about to be shipped off to Korea. He went on about how much he would love to be picked for that night's show so his folks could watch him. Not being able to tell him about my having been pre-selected, I felt horribly guilty and would have given anything to let him take my place. He beamed when I was led off to meet Groucho, but to me the whole thing had lost its sparkle. I've often wondered what happened to him.

My co-contestant was a young moving man, and Groucho had all the jokes ready about his moving the "Danish pastry." I was somewhat disillusioned to see him reading his lines off a prompter's screen and terrified that I'd forget my cues. It was even worse when he deviated from the script, though he very neatly got me back on the track each time. I wanted "Geography" as the quiz category, but the moving man chose "Vocabulary." This being before Women's Lib, he won. I had never heard any of the words they questioned me about, and the moving man wasn't faring much better. Our downfall was "pediatrician," which I still think should have something to do with feet! Back in the co-op we had already optimistically planned what to do with the loot, even if I won only the minimal amount, so it was a droopy-eared celebrity who crept home that night with empty pockets.

Christmas was getting close, yet the palm trees were still waving and the weather was balmy. The Christmas spirit seemed to melt in the hot sun. To chase it away even further, pink and baby blue plastic trees appeared with colored bulbs flashing on and off, a far cry from snow-covered streets, noses pressed against frozen candle-lit windows and the smell of baking and pine trees. Oh, did I feel homesick. The Israeli girl, who didn't celebrate Christmas anyway, a Puerto Rican girl and I, plus two stray cats, were all that were left in the clapboard. I'd had invitations for Christmas but I just didn't feel like accepting them. One note of "Silent Night" would have sent me into a flood of tears, and nobody was to watch my misery.

We had exactly seventy-eight cents among us, plus various leftovers in the fridge. It was worse than Dicken's *Christmas*

Carol before Scrooge got religion. With her usual through-ness, my mother's Christmas gifts and check had arrived in November and had long since been opened and used. To make matters worse, I had read O. Henry's "Gift of The Magi," and that had really finished me off. In Denmark we always talk about "the uncle from America," that is, the rich unknown uncle from whom you suddenly inherit a vast fortune or whatever. On that Christmas Eve afternoon, he reared his beautiful head. A letter arrived from Chicago from an uncle who faithfully had forgotten my existence for years. Enclosed was a check for fifty dollars. Thank God he'd forgotten me until now! We didn't walk, we *ran* to the nearest supermarket and then to the drugstore. Candles, wine, food, whatever present we could think of for each other at that late hour . . . I swear it was almost snowing when we got home!

By spring I was really involved in campus life and becoming more American than the Americans. I had changed room-mates and my present one was a lovely black girl, very light of skin. One night one of the older girls in the co-op asked us if we would like to go to a lesbian bar. I had no idea what that meant (and was too shy to ask) but knew from her tone of voice it would be something out of the ordinary. It turned out to be a dingy, dimly lit spot where, to our embarrassment, we ran into two fellows from the university who promptly asked my roommate and me for a date. We arranged that they'd pick us up at the house the next evening. Our dates arrived and walked into the parlor, took one look at my roommate and stalked out. Needless to say, they were white and had not realized her color in the darkness of the bar. Her reaction was terrifying to watch and I felt very helpless. It was my first direct contact with the racial problem in the U.S., completely beyond my comprehension. I can still see her standing in the bathroom looking at herself in the mirror and screaming her protest at the whole world.

I had a friend in the film department who insisted that my future lay in movies. I'd never heard such a load of nonsense in all my life, but to pacify this persistent individual and satisfy a vague curiosity (after all, "movieland" was just around the

73

corner), I agreed to see one of the big Hollywood agents with whom my friend set up a meeting. Had I not been so incredibly ignorant of the industry and its machinations, I might have been more impressed, awed or frightened. As it was, it was merely like a dental appointment and in this case it was a necessity to please my friend. We were led into an enormous, luxuriously appointed room with the biggest desk I'd ever seen, behind which sat the smallest man, busily talking on the phone. He never looked up to acknowledge my presence but just kept on talking. I thought that was extremely bad manners and was put off immediately. When he finally got around to talking to me the conversation that followed was rather bizarre:

"Have you had any experience in the theatre or in the movies?"

"No."

"Have you had any theatrical training at all?"

"No."

"Would you be interested in becoming a movie star?"

"No."

"Then why are you here?"

"I don't really know."

He looked absolutely perplexed, my friend dejected and I relieved, and that was the signal for departure.

My cinema friend managed to con me once more. We went to a major studio where I felt I was being paraded like a side of beef, undressed by their eyes. Perhaps I was being presumptuous, but I felt insulted by the whole thing and couldn't wait to get out of there. I was majoring in education, not illusions—little did I know I'd be back to deal in those same illusions twenty years later.

I began to think seriously about staying at U.S.C. a second year. Although my tuitional grant could easily be extended, my financial situation was still precarious. Salvation came when I was invited to pledge. This was a side of campus life of which I'd seen very little. I knew the honorary societies and was a member of a few, but had only been inside several of the sororities the first days of my arrival the previous fall. This, too, would be a valuable experience and, when they offered me room and board for the following year, which I never could have afforded otherwise, I accepted.

After the unbelievable mad whirl of "rushing," I chose Pi Beta Phi and, luckily, they chose me, too. I couldn't get over the luxury and comfort of the sorority houses. The girls were incredibly friendly and helpful, but now I had to give up the one piece of individuality I had stubbornly held on to—namely, my large golden earrings, but the exchange was okay with me. Here again I marveled at the initiative and self-confidence everyone had, the way everybody was involved with the campus organizations and just doing things, and in that respect, felt very inadequate and very young. Only slowly did I realize the power of organizations and became very team-oriented, too. It's very contagious.

I must put down my honest recollections of initiation, hopefully without sounding ungrateful. One of my fellow pledges was Marilyn Horne, the now world-famous mezzo-soprano. She had twinkling blue eyes full of mischief and humor and a marvelously gutsy laugh. Although we never said it straight out to each other, I had a feeling she found initiation as campy as I. Such flurry and excitement. Stately elderly Pi Phi alumnae flapping about in white robes, and much secrecy in waiting. I remember the two of us looking at ourselves in the shower room and donning our white vestal virgin outfits. What the mirror reflected looked like two fallen angels. We were blindfolded and led into the candlelit assembly room accompanied by the sentimental snuffles of the old alums to swear our undying devotion to the lofty aims and ideals of the sisterhood, the arrow and the "Wine and Blue."

I fully appreciated the function of social organizations on a campus as large as U.S.C., and the various charities they individually supported were extremely worthy causes. However, why shouldn't I be sisterly to everyone? This sisterhood business seemed to exclude everybody except Pi Phi from being near-perfect. Was the test money or religion? What was the standard? Besides, yellow is my favorite color, and I knew nothing about archery! When all the formalities were finished,

75

we could finally relax, and I truly looked forward to returning in the fall.

My parents arrived at term's end to take me back to Denmark. I looked too striped and star-spangled for their taste. But, no way! The compromise effected was that I'd go with them on a freighter to Canada and they'd let me off on their way back, which they did. There was still a lot of summer left and, again, the limitations on my student visa as to the types of job I could take. So when my Santa Barbara friends suggested a job taking care of an only child who lived right on the beach, I jumped at the opportunity. The idea of being someone else's nanny rather tickled my sense of humor, and the thought of being by the sea clinched it for me.

Terry was eight or nine and very much in need of a friend, as her parents were in the throes of a painful divorce. We got along just fine, playing, studying, and swimming together, and I got paid sixty dollars a month plus room and board. The weeks flowed by smoothly, and then came the night of the earthquake.

Just before dawn, I awoke suddenly to a deep rumbling like that of an underground train. The house was shaking and rattling, and things started crashing down from tables and shelves. Terry was screaming hysterically in her bed across the room. I tried to get up, but kept tumbling back. All I could do was hang on to the sides of my bed, which was rocking like a small boat in a storm. Curtains were standing at an angle into the room, water was slopping out of the dog's bowl and glass was splintering in the bathroom. It seemed to last an eternity and then—sudden silence. Terry dashed over to my bed and both of us crawled under the blankets.

I was at least as scared as she was. Too late did I remember advice I'd read to stand in a doorway or go outside. It was much better playing ostrich. There were two or three more jolts, but at last it subsided. It still took several minutes for the two of us to reassure each other that the thing was over. At last we crept out to view the shambles and spent the rest of the dawn hours drinking coffee and chocolate milk to steady our nerves. Later, the cook told us that a small town, Taha-

76

chopee, had been completely destroyed by the same earthquake, one of the worst California had experienced in a very
long time.

However, that morning we went to the beach for an early
swimming lesson. I was walking beside Terry, supporting her
as she practiced her arm strokes. Suddenly, I stepped into a
void and plunged under. I came up, caught her immediately
and then searched for the bottom. There wasn't any.

Terry was thrashing about practically strangling me in her
terror, and it took several minutes to convince her that we
would get safely back to shore. With her hanging on to my
back and relaxing as best she could, I started swimming back,
suddenly realizing we were much farther out than we'd been
when the bottom had vanished. Clearly, we were in one of
those treacherous currents I'd been warned about. It was carrying us out to sea. Hoping Terry wouldn't notice this, I began
to swim at an inward angle down the coast as I'd been taught
to do years ago in Copenhagen.

It seemed I was swimming hours in the water, but it was
probably not more than fifteen or twenty minutes, with pauses
only to reassure Terry that all was well. I have always been a
strong swimmer, but I began to worry seriously as the minutes
dragged by and the shore seemed no closer. It was still very
early in the morning, the beach was deserted, and it would be
hours before we were missed. My visions were of the two of
us floating in, bloated and horrible like that German soldier
of my childhood. Finally, when my arms were beginning to
weigh hundreds of pounds and my lungs were aching, I saw
that we'd make it. In a few more strokes, I stuck a toe down
and brushed sand; in a few more, I was standing, holding
Terry by the hand and gasping for breath. The sea bed had
obviously changed contours during the earthquake the night
before.

As we walked up the beach toward home, I looked out at
the immense and peaceful ocean. I had met fear of the sea for
the first time, I loved it no less, but had learned that it could
be indifferently cruel to the insignificant specks that entered
it.

That afternoon the damages were also visible in Santa Barbara: buildings had cracked, windows were broken and, going to the local supermarket, we waded in a foot-and-a-half of dill pickles, apricot preserves, Coca-Cola and catsup, with an armada of boxes and other objects floating through the aisles. If it hadn't been for the grocer's financial loss, the sight would have been priceless.

I stayed with Terry through July and August, saving my pay, and at the end of the summer had enough to buy a third-class train ticket to New York, by way of the Grand Canyon and Chicago.

The Grand Canyon is one of the truly awesome sights in the world. I still recall the emotional impact of seeing the bottom of the Canyon. During the day I spent there I fed the chipmunks and sat on a boulder till the sun went down watching the reddish rocks of the Canyon walls melting into a deep purple. The scale is impossible to grasp, like a *trompe d'oeil* painting in which tricks are played with perspective. The greenery seems at times to be fairly close, like bushes seen from a castle wall, and then a blink of the eye reveals them to be huge trees thousands of feet below. Once I dropped a rock over the edge and listened for what must have been several minutes for the clunk—which I never heard.

I still do this often: sit on a hillside, sit on a quiet beach, sit on a parkbench, but alone. One can dream, one can think, get everything into perspective—one rests one's spirit.

Back on the train the next day for the long trip through the flat farmlands to Chicago. I had only a few hours during the stopover there, but did squeeze in an exploration of the area around the station and my first and hopefully last experience downwind of the slaughterhouses.

Just as the monotony of the New York run was threatening my spine and my sanity, I met two girls from Wisconsin who were also heading East for a sightseeing visit. We chattered the day away, in our seats and in the dining car, and the time flew.

Then night came. Jane and Laura returned to their own seats to get what sleep they could, and I sat there staring at the black window and occasional flashes of passing lights, hoping to find at least a few hours of rest. Just as I was dozing off, something landed in my lap. It was a foot! Two of them, in fact. They belonged to a large man who'd been nipping from a bottle all day and who was now snoring drunkenly in the opposite seat. I sat there rigidly, praying he'd realize his mistake, trying to summon up the courage to wake him and protest. Ultimately, I stared at those damned enormous feet in impotent rage. Incredible as it seems, he snored on and those fifty-pound feet stayed in my lap the entire night while I sat there, aches and pains and then numbness spreading through most of my body, too timid to wake him. Not until sometime after dawn did he grunt a few times, snort, and finally shift so that the feet slid to the floor. I stood up and tried to straighten my back, feeling like the granny in the rocking chair, and staggered like a robot down the aisle to the loo.

At last I arrived in Grand Central Station, feeling years older than when I'd left Los Angeles. I found Jane and Laura again, and we went off to enjoy one of New York's summertime specialties: a heat wave that could melt your bridgework, combined with steam-bath humidity and foul-smelling, unmoving air. Nonetheless, I loved the place, although I do remember walking up Fifth Avenue at rush hour thinking, "I could drop dead, just keel over, and nobody would stop or take any notice."

The three of us spent a week zipping about. We went to the top of the Empire State Building but I never left the lift, hating heights even more than the seven vertical mal-de-mer trips I took up and down waiting for Jane and Laura. We covered Manhattan from the Cloisters to the Staten Island Ferry, tried on the latest fashions, which none of us could afford, and dined in wonderful restaurants of every ethnic flavor imaginable. We were, as only young girls on such a lark could be, completely oblivious to the ninety-five-degree stickiness that occupied ninety-nine percent of the conversations around us.

The trip back to California was enlivened by chats with fellow passengers who, upon hearing I was a foreigner, began asking questions in the straight-forward manner characteristic of most Americans. To a lot of Europeans, this insatiable curiosity and blunt questioning seem to reveal a lack of finesse and considerable ignorance. I've often wondered: perhaps we Europeans are just hypocritical in our fear of betraying our ignorance and appearing stupid. We just keep silent and nod our heads with a knowing smile, even if we don't know.

Back at the Pi Phi house, Marilyn, Sally, Josie and I were assigned the only room on the second floor aside from the assembly room. It wasn't a large room by any means but nevertheless was pleasantly private and isolated. We flipped coins for beds (mine next to the window was happily compatible with my eiderdown from home), but Marilyn's and my real concern was where to hide our gallon of California white wine. I was used to having a glass of wine at dinner from the age of fourteen, as my stepfather's theory was that a lady had to learn how to hold her liquor. Besides he felt, and I wholly agree, that no meal was civilized without wine. He also wished all kinds of hell-fire and damnation to be rained down on those who instigated the practice of putting plastic corks into champagne bottles—progress had progressed too far.

We decided upon the wastebasket, much to the amusement of the lady who cleaned the room, and for the rest of the year a big bottle of California Chablis nestled there under carefully arranged trash, undisturbed by the maid.

The second year passed much too quickly. I finally got the hang of American football, which I had formerly dismissed as a total bore. My initial reaction after a lifetime exposure to European soccer, was that all one saw were huge gorilla-like multicolored shapes piling on top of each other. They'd fight over something that was kept a secret until at last it came flying through the legs of one of them, upon which they'd all rise and unfold like a giant sea anemone and start haring down the field after the flying object. Or, nothing would happen and they'd just flop there in a very large heap. Every twenty minutes, the heap was moved a couple of yards this way or a couple of yards that way. So much for football.

There were classes and dates and evenings reading and talking in our room. Since Marilyn Horne sang with the Roger

Wagner Chorale, she had an all-night pass and was envied by all. I've rejoiced at her great success over the years. She was one of the funniest story tellers I've ever known, and always came home with a bag of new stories and jokes that would keep us up half the night.

I was busy on all fronts and extremely happy, and if there was some doubt about how much those college years broadened my mind, there was absolutely no doubt about their broadening effect on the rest of me. Rounder and more *softig* each month, by spring my figure had achieved something near the proportions of a Wagnerian soprano, without the voice.

Once on a blind date, I was paired off with a basketball player. He was not quite the height of Wilt Chamberlain, but no more than half his width. My first thought upon confronting him was: here we are, Abbott and Costello in co-ed version. If it hadn't been that my size was a crying matter, I would have burst out laughing. After that humiliation I gave up the dating game and turned elsewhere for diversion, working with the Little Theater group and on the Varsity Show, but backstage as usual.

As final exams neared, I got a letter from my old friend Bee, who was then living with her husband in Cuba. She asked me to visit them in May, before they moved on to another part of the world. Credits from an American university were useless in Denmark, since in Denmark one merely attends classes until he feels educated and courageous enough to try the exams, usually taking six or seven years for a master's degree. So, I decided: "Never mind the credits, I hopefully have the knowledge"—and jumped on a plane for Havana.

Getting off the plane was more of a stagger—into the hottest blanket of air I'd ever encountered. Equally hot was the gossip about a high government official who disappeared with the entire contents of the postal widows' pension fund. This seemed to be an unusual occurrence, even in the Battista regime, and Havana buzzed about it for weeks.

Bee, my hostess, and I tried the beach a few times, where I received my first lessons in snorkeling—within the shark nets —and my first sunburn and ensuing freckles, much to my mother's everlasting horror. Most of the time, however, the heat drove us back to Bee's flat, where we lolled about in loose pajama tops and sipped rum punch to ease the pain of the sunburn. There were many reminiscences about our childhood together in school and about her older brother. He had given me my first kiss at age fourteen under the mistletoe we'd chosen—purely for ulterior motives—as a Christmas greeting for her mother. Bee's brother had also greatly added to our education when he returned from four years at Andover Academy with a vocabulary that far exceeded the English we'd learned in the classroom. One word he taught us he refused to define, and we suspected it might be something not normally used in everyday conversation with one's mother. But it had a nice gutsy ring to it and popped out from time to time. During a visit to the American Embassy in Finland, where Bee had once spent a summer holiday, she was dressing for the evening's ball and found the zipper on her dress had stuck. She opened her door and found a young man in the hallway, to whom she sweetly addressed these now famous words: "I can't get this fucking zipper up. Could you help me, please?"

The young man stared at her, politely helped her with the zipper, then went on to admonish her that this was not a word to be used by well-bred young Danish ladies. To insure that her English got proper guidance, he married her after her year at Bryn Mawr and took her back to America. Then he moved her to Cuba, where she had the opportunity to relearn all the most colorful phrases in Spanish.

I've never been able to understand why swearing and profanity in a foreign language don't bother me, yet similar phrases in Danish I find offensive.

Bee and I sipped rum, reminisced some more, and made occasional forays into Havana's night life with her husband. We nearly drove him crazy with our giggles and Danish. But now the letters from Copenhagen were beginning to sound a bit curt and impatient. I decided I had better heed them, so I ruefully said my goodbyes and boarded a KLM plane for the endless flight home, via Newfoundland and Shannon. In this pre-jet time the flights were truly grueling.

82

This was a period of intense competition among airlines, each trying to outdo the others to win passenger love and approval. We had dinner, we were given cheese, then we were awakened every few minutes and bombarded with souvenirs: little wooden shoes, boxes of chocolates, miniature bottles of Genever, the Dutch aquavit. Finally, in the middle of my third or fourth breakfast, I dozed off, only to be awakened somewhere over Newfoundland by the stewardess with yet another souvenir of Holland—and I still had that last big mouthful of scrambled eggs intact in my mouth.

At last the plane landed, and I stumbled a bit reluctantly down the steps to a Copenhagen I'd not seen for two years.

Nora Élé

*"Il canto é la luce, un mondo d'amore
ma senza affanni."*

If it weren't for the beauty of youth, they
would be intolerable! I think it was Shaw who
said it, and intolerable I was, enhanced by my questionable
beauty now weighing in at 140 pounds.

After two years in America, the pace of Copenhagen to me
was like a snail's. Most of my friends had left, were studying
seriously or had married, moving into spheres of concern
quite alien to my own. The social life I had known—the weekend parties, the elegant balls—now belonged to a younger set,
my sister's, into which a world-weary sophisticate of twenty-
one just didn't fit.

Even Sussi's and my basic life styles clashed. Her room, for
instance, was bright and neat and full of horses—statues of
them, pictures of them, the jumpers even leapt out of the
wallpaper. It was, in every way, the typical room of a typical
teen-ager, right out of *House Beautiful.*

My own room, on the other hand, was an unorganized
rummage sale: clothes knee-deep, books, magazines, junk of
every sort. I lived in and added to this rat's nest for months

before finally digging in to rediscover the rug. My mother, of course, was horrified by this sulky, restless creature who'd once been her daughter, but she somehow held her tongue until the mess became unbearable. "I feel sorry for your poor husband, if you ever get one the way you're acting," she sighed, and quietly insisted that something had to be done about it—and me. This, naturally, was proof-positive of how little they all understood me.

Even more galling was money. After two years of self-sufficiency in America, having to ask my parents for a handout for a movie, a new sweater or what-have-you both irritated and humiliated me. As generous as they were, I always felt like a six-year-old scrounging a penny for the candy lady. The idea of taking a part-time job didn't occur to me, mainly because there was no such thing. One worked fulltime at his trade or profession or apprenticed oneself to a professional to learn a trade. The American custom of hiring college-age kids for part-time work was unknown in Denmark.

A few sessions of practice-teaching in California had killed the idea of entering *that* profession. The children had been noisy, answered the teachers back and were complete brats, a situation unthinkable in the discipline of the Danish schools I had attended. If this was the coming thing in education, I wanted no part of it. With that attitude, there seemed little point in returning to a university to pursue a degree in teaching.

The real burr under the saddle was the aimlessness I'd felt since stepping off the plane. What the devil was I doing here? What *could* I do here?

I moped. When golf became a bore, there was tennis, and when that palled, there was sailing and a brief romance with cars. We owned several, and I used to race an old wooden station wagon up and down the coast, visiting friends, taxiing houseguests to and from the station—but that, too, became a bore. Then I'd just sit on the terrace like an ugly black cloud, watching the same old faces drinking the same old cider and black currant juice, trying to stifle a scream of frustration.

What really pulled me out of my self-made bog was looking

up Eleanora Rasmussen, or Nora Élé, as she'd been known professionally (she often said that, in *her* day, one just could not be a famous soprano and be called *Rasmussen*). A frail sparrow of a woman in her early seventies with the wisdom of a guru and the patience of a saint, she'd years before given me voice lessons. I had loved singing in her choir, and she had often been in my thoughts since then. She was devoted to music and to anyone gifted with what she called "the most divine instrument of all," a beautiful voice.

"It is the *smallest* instrument of all," she once told me, "but it is the one that pierces the clearest and goes straight into the soul." She believed the human voice to be a true miracle. How else, she'd ask, could the sound produced by those two tiny bits of living flesh and the breath carry clearly above an entire symphony orchestra?

Élé, as we all called her, was a widow, having been married to a painter with whom she'd lived in Rome. After his premature death, she had turned all her talents and energies to teaching, at which she was outstanding, but it was as a human being that she was the real teacher.

Although I hadn't the remotest idea of a musical career, some fateful hand pushed me out of bed one morning and over to see her. After our initial reunion, it seemed entirely natural that we just start in where we'd left off years before, as if the lessons had merely hung in some limbo waiting to be reclaimed. For the first time in all the miserable months I'd been home, I had something to do, something I could really get involved with, and it gave me a sense of happy energy I'd not known since California.

After the first couple of weeks, Élé moved from her tiny rooms to a big sunny flat in the old section of Copenhagen. This was an "honorary house," with rent-free flats given to retired or semi-retired people of the arts as a reward for their contributions to the country's cultural life. As much as the building attracted these performers, the district drew dozens of streetwalkers shouting out their prices to all male passers-by. Each time I went to see her, I wondered what this delicate, dainty lady must think of the terrible commotion and its cause.

One day when I arrived, she seemed a bit upset. I asked her what was wrong.

"It's those girls out there," she gestured. "I think it's just awful!"

Uh, oh, I thought. Here it comes.

"Last night I was leaning out my window waiting for a friend to arrive," she continued, "and I heard those girls calling out their prices to the men. I listened for quite a while and finally couldn't stan it any more. So I leaned out farther and yelled down at one of them, 'My dear, you are selling youself much too cheaply. You're worth twice what you're asking . . . you're just degrading your own sex!' "

So much for the sheltered sensibilities of a seventy-year-old lady!

In her eyes, there was beauty in everything, and she could talk about everyday things and make them seem very special. Her intuition was incredible—she instinctively knew when one was troubled and why. Through a parable or a simple story, she'd suddenly resolve one's problem of the moment without ever having heard a word of it.

One of Élé's musical theories was that a big voice should not be cramped into a tiny body, but should have spacious quarters. My own voice was currently living in a veritable palace. Thanks to a mild metabolic imbalance aggravated by too many eating-out-of-boredom raids on the kitchen, the padding I'd added at U.S.C. had been fleshed out even more. But Élé was right: my voice was bigger then than it has ever been since.

It was she who introduced me to the classics, my home not having been especially musical. She had taken me to a chamber music recital when I was thirteen, and now we regularly attended the opera. No matter the performance, there was always an uncanny feeling of hearing it all through her ears, sensing and understanding things I could not have appreciated on my own. She never explained, she simply listened, with an intensity and devotion that made the whole thing quite magical for me. This intensity was part of everything she did—one could not help but feel an almost electric sense of *life* in her presence.

My voice improved steadily, and Élé became more and more convinced that I was destined for a career in serious music. I loved these times with her, I loved singing, but other problems within myself made me reluctant to make a whole-hearted commitment.

I was living in an emotional No-Man's-Land. Although I lived at home and, gratingly, was still as dependent as a child, I no longer felt a child's sense of belonging in the family circle. Most of my time at the house was spent locked away in my "nest" at the top of the tower, reading, eating, practicing scales, and emerging only for midnight forays into library or pantry. And for at least the first five months of my lessons, I let no one hear me practice.

I did overcome that painful self-consciousness long enough to give a brief one-girl recital. It hadn't seemed fair that Mother should pay for all those lessons without having one whit of proof that they were doing any good. Shoveling away piles of the now-accustomed debris into closets, under the bed, God knows where, I invited her and my stepfather into my room, sitting them in chairs that hadn't seen the light of day since my return. Élé was at the old upright, and I went through "Butterfly," "Tales of Hoffman," "La Bohême" and what have you, and I think truly impressed them. At any rate Mother didn't flinch at the suggestion of further training in Italy when Élé brought it up in the early spring.

Élé felt, after six months, that I had gone as far with her as I could and most definitely should continue my studies with one of the really fine teachers in Italy, to prepare for a career in opera. As deeply flattered as I was, the idea of doing so created a tremendous battle with my conscience. Could I be a professional performer when I was too shy to let even my own family hear me sing? The mere thought of going on stage made me shake. Could I stand the years of dependence on my family while I studied?

For weeks I was torn between the horns of the dilemma: I was devoted to my singing and to the lady who'd been both benefactress and friend in developing it, but I was stifled by the dullness of Copenhagen, the terror of performing publicly and, worst of all, the endless dependence on my parents. Finally, I made my decision. I'd give up music and go to Paris.

At last I'd be off on my own once again, taking classes at L'Alliance Française and attending lectures at the Sorbonne, but most important, just *being* in Paris, a free spirit in the city I'd always dreamed of. My mother, surprisingly, agreed, though I see in retrospect she was probably delighted that an end to all the grumbling and grousing was in sight. With a small inheritance I'd received at twenty-one in my pocket, I purchased a second-class rail ticket to Paris. One way.

I deliberately busied myself in packing, tidying up, almost any odd chore to put off the painful experience of telling Élé my decision. Finally I worked up enough courage and went to see her. The worst thing was that I knew she would understand completely and would bury her own disappointments in her wishes for my happiness. It was painful as we sat sipping tea, crying a little and trying to cheer each other up, and then I sang her two most favorite songs. I fled immediately, hating myself for having hurt her.

The next day my mother drove me, my luggage and my guitar to the station. She shook her head sadly as I boarded the train, heaving a big sigh which must have been partly in relief. The last thing I heard her say was, "Well, at least I suppose you'll learn to speak French."

$\mathcal{P}aris$

Had there been a raging blizzard, it wouldn't have mattered—but it was springtime, the countryside looked very green, very French, and the moment the train pulled into the Gare du Nord could not have been more exhilarating.

My mental image of life in Paris had been well-formed from years of poring over history books, magazines and papers, and taking in every French film wherever I was. I'd packed accordingly: black sweaters, black pants, black tights and a guitar for the Left Bank; ball gowns, the inevitable gloves and a list of family friends for the Right Bank. The decision was easy: to hell with family friends' surveillance and reports home, at least for the moment.

I got my feet on the ground just long enough that afternoon to find a room in a dingy hotel on Rue du Monsieur le Prince. What it lacked in charm, it more than made up for in drabness, but it was cheap, clean, full of Americans (a most welcome sight) and as good a place as any to leave my schizophrenic wardrobe and prowl the city.

Can anyone truly describe the emotion of realizing a long-held dream when its reality is even more wonderful than one had ever dared hope? In the eyes of a twenty-two-year-old

90

romantic savoring the first real freedom of her life, Paris was headier than a magnum of Dom Perignon. I walked everywhere and anywhere those first two weeks, with guidebook but no plan, still not quite believing it wasn't a dream. Paris is the only city I know where, as you watch the hustle and bustle of the twentieth century, you also have constant historical imagery passing before your eyes.

Night and day I ambled and strolled until my blistered feet gave out . . . staring bug-eyed at the elegant rows of shops on Rue Faubourg, St. Hônoré, Rue de Rivoli and on past L'Opèra, where later I would sit in the balcony where the most enthusiastic crowd always sat . . . Avenue Montaigne and Avenue Matignon, where the salons of the haute couturiers were discreetly announced by a simple brass plaque, all very forbidding . . . low stone archways opening into small treed and flowered courtyards filled with even more boutiques and tiny galleries . . . the Ritz, whose American Bar had been the focal point of so many of my Paris readings, but which then intimidated me.

The commerce of the Left Bank was just as captivating . . . the open-air markets just off Boulevard Saint Germain, where berets and white aprons haggled with kerchiefs and string shopping bags over a jumble of charcuterie, asparagus, skinned rabbits and sole . . . the delicious sight of an errand-running six-year-old in knee pants, his right arm crooked about a sack of greens, his left holding a three-foot loaf of freshly baked bread, the end of which he solemnly nibbled as he walked home . . . groups of giggling little schoolboys in their blue and white checked smocks weighed down by huge bundles of books slung over their shoulders by a leather strap. And, of course, there were the sidewalk cafés, where I'd drop into a chair with a delighted tiredness, enlarging my very limited French vocabulary by at least two words a day in chats with the waiters. As weary as I was, the happy mix of chess players, girl watchers, matrons with their bundles, solitary readers, students between classes and a May-and-December romance in the corner made my *vin ordinaire* pure ambrosia.

I took predawn strolls through Les Halles, sidestepping

91

mountains of cabbages, dodging trucks piled high with crates of ill-fated chickens, inhaling all the marvelous smells of fresh produce as I followed my nose to a crock of the justifiably famous onion soup.

My very rusty academic French was good enough to laugh in the Bois de Boulogne at a noon-day spring sun worshipper propped up against an *"Interdite Sur La Pelouse"* sign, though hardly adequate to follow a heated sidewalk political debate in the Student Quarter. Still, the fervor of the two young men lost nothing in translation. And there was the Seine, along which I walked for hours. It was fascinating any time of day, but I especially liked to sit beside it at dusk, when the lights from the river barges, their laundry still flapping, and from the *bateaux mouches* came on. With chestnut trees just in bloom, lovers strolling past the kiosks, *clochards* looking for that night's shelter under the bridges, it was at twilight a living impressionistic painting.

The one thing that made me know I indeed was not dreaming was my first look at the Eiffel Tower. That first glimpse stopped me dead in my tracks: I think it's the ugliest oversized erector set any architect has ever put together, but of course, you can't ignore it.

Though the time spent in my hotel was obviously minimal —a few hours' sleep and a change of clothes—its transient population was too noisy and my privacy infringed upon constantly. There was a twenty-four hour party going on and studying was impossible against a background of clinking glasses and bottles. It was time to move. The student advisory office at the Sorbonne had long lists of cheap accommodations and I began to check them out, whizzing through the city on the back of a German student's motor scooter. Most places were more horrid than where I was—lots of people apparently figured to make a few easy francs renting out space, not even suitable for the family dog, to desperate economy-minded students. But finally I moved into a large flat on Avenue de Saxe. Actually, a family named Cornichon had the flat; I rented one room and the use of the bathtub once a week, for about 3,000 old francs. The place was in an old-fashioned bourgeoisie part of the 7th Arrondisement, quite close to the Sorbonne, and done in faded Victorian plush complete with antimacassars and flowered carpet.

My room gave me my first jolting experience with the color combination of bright orange and shocking pink, albeit also faded, in an unthinkable flowered wallpaper. There was a huge bed, a few pieces of mismatched furniture and a window looking onto a narrow street of more gray buildings. And the bath situation—the tub, a big old-fashioned claw-footed thing, was almost always full of laundry. When it finally was emptied, usually toward the end of the week, a gurgling electric water heater overhead gave forth no more than a trickle of hot water. The Cornichons often went away on Thursdays for the weekend, and I could have cheated and had more than one bath then, but I was always afraid they'd read the meter and toss me out. The French can be frugal to the point of madness.

I was also allowed to use the family kitchen to make a cup of tea and, again, could have done much more elaborate cooking in their weekend absences. However, the extent of their cleanliness hardly matched that of their frugality (they'd frequently take off Thursday nights leaving all the dirty dishes and half-eaten food right on the table), so tea was about it. But they were very kind and solicitous and most curious in a friendly way about my origins and earlier exploits.

Although it was early springtime, the nights in my room were so cold that I used to curl up in my blankets, sweater and overcoat with the little chamois bag holding my first three months' allowance under my pillow. During the day I wore the bag around my neck (Mother's idea: she was convinced that Paris was filled with unsavory characters bent upon snatching away my money—and my virtue).

The French I'd studied for years in school was of little help when it came to speaking it now. Although I was enrolled in the Sorbonne and regularly attended lectures in French civilization, art and culture, I didn't understand a word of it. However, the experience *was* marvelous for attuning the ear to the rhythms and inflections of the language, a great help when I studied it at the Alliance Française. Because of this void in

93

spoken French, plus my feeling very comfortable in California-style English, most of my friends were American students spending a year or two abroad, in addition to Irene, a childhood friend from Copenhagen.

Irene was in Paris for only a few months, living in a very good arrondisement in what appeared to be a "good" flat but which, in fact, looked out on a rear yard infested with rats. Sometimes from the safety of her windows on a sluggish Saturday morning with nothing better to do, we'd each pick a speedy-looking rat and bet on which would cross the dump first.

Saturday was also the day she and I would sit down and divide our allowances into weekly spending expenses, (God, how I hated the months with thirty-one days). We'd subtract our mandatory expenses, like carfare and rent, then budget a minimal amount for food and our gallons of coffee. The rest was for opera, theatre, clothes, personal needs, graphics and drawings or whatever. That sounds pretty sensible, I suppose, but the key words were "minimal amount of food." When we were on our own; that is, without dates, the intake was black coffee and, if we were desperate, one croissant. I still can't look at a croissant without thinking of our regular haunt, the Café aux Deux Magots, where the waiters always put a heaping but pre-counted plate of them on the table, then charged for the ones eaten. With our being on an "emergency ration" of just one each, the others seemed to get bigger and lighter and flakier until we had to beg to have them removed.

Over many cups of coffee, Irene and I also figured how to scrounge as many free dinners as possible. If one of us had a dinner date, she'd suggest to her beau that they make it a foursome and find a date for the other. Once at the table, we'd both eat as if we hadn't seen a decent meal for days which, of course, was absolutely true. Our mothers would have winced at our immodesty, having taught us always to select the lowest-priced item on the menu, pretending, of course, not to have seen the prices at all. This was most becoming for young ladies, but they never said anything about having seconds. To this day I cannot sit down in a restaurant, be the host most

94

well-to-do or not, without instinctively looking for the cheapest dish. And, as far as ordering the most expensive, it would have to be suggested and I persuaded—and I'd still have a guilty conscience. How's that for indoctrination!

At one point, I did buy a student restaurant ticket at the Sorbonne. But the constant serving of tripe, a food that completely belies all the delectable things the French do with food, got me out of that economy move in a hurry. There was always a supply of cheese and wine in our rooms, and splurges on *beignets* and cocoa for special occasions. Through this self-imposed austerity program, I not only managed to set aside extra money for new guitar strings or more black tights, but also lost all my fat from college and Copenhagen. Mother, on her few visits, wondered at the sudden skinniness and had her suspicions when, with such ease, she could coax me into some of her favorite "four-forks-and-knives" restaurants and watch me go through a five-course dinner.

I made two rather startling ethnic discoveries that spring. Often taken for an American because of my linguistic preferences, I still never realized how detested the Americans were in Paris until a car I'd borrowed broke down one evening. My first attempts to find help were greeted with contempt and derision. Only after pulling out and waving a tiny Danish flag I always carried with me, coloring my English with a very strained Danish accent, and putting on the helpless female act did the garage door open up. And, lo and behold, the repairs were free of charge.

In direct contradiction to that was the amazing discovery that Scandinavian girls were generally regarded as a sexual smørgasbord, available for sampling at any time. Indeed, the university dormitory that housed the Scandinavian girls was laughingly known as "The Baby Factory." In my sheltered adolescence, I had never encountered this apparently popular belief, and there had been too few of us in California for that attitude to take root. Nevertheless, to say in Paris that one was Danish was practically to invite rape.

One time that spring I queued for twenty-eight hours in front of L'Opèra to get tickets for the first western performance of the Bolshoi. Two feet from the box office I fainted, and woke up across the street in a café, its proprietor anxiously pouring cognac down my throat. The policeman who'd brought me there left, then returned and, with a flourish, presented me with my wallet and the tickets he'd bought for the performances. How's that for French gallantry? After all that, the performance was canceled a few days later due to a change in the political climate, but my parsimony never stretched far enough to endure another twenty-eight hours for a refund.

My stepfather, an avid sportsman, loved Paris and when there, always visited the "Tir aux Pigeons," an exclusive shooting club in the Bois de Boulogne. I had long enjoyed shooting galleries at fun fairs, but this was a different kettle of fish. The targets were live pigeons or clay discs. At the time, however, I gave very little thought to the fate of the poor pigeons and definitely developed a killer instinct. My first effort was as a contestant in a match for couples. I had never held a .12-gauge shotgun before and very nonchalantly threw it to my shoulder and yelled, "Pull!" Both barrels went off at once, and I was flung at least three feet backward, almost landing on my tail. The pain was acute but I laughed, determined to impress my partner with whom I had instantly fallen in love, an affliction that was to last a very, very long time.

Charles had the most incredible eyes I've ever seen: green with brown flecks and always smiling with a certain sparkle. He was a bit taller than I, athletic and elegant, always impeccably dressed and with an inner warmth, something I usually found lacking in the oftimes cynical French. Maybe it was due to his mother's Polish origins. I fell and stayed felled. . . .

We saw each other during the next two months, often driving out to the club for an afternoon's shooting or sitting in the family box at the races at Longchamps. Since I didn't have a hat of my own, I went to see an old friend from Denmark who now was working for Jacques Fath. My mother had been one of his first clients when he opened his hat shop in Copenhagen, and now that he was with M. Fath, he reciprocated her patronage by lending me any hat from the collection. He also pro-

96

y younger sister Sussi and I in
apallo just after my father's death
1936.

Still sulking from a scolding by my mother when
this birthday picture was taken at age six.

y father, Kaj Møller, was an Eng-
h barrister before becoming the
wspaper publisher in Copen-
agen.

age three: a photo my father especially
ed and carried.

My mother, Clara Hasselbalch, always
lovely looking, on her way to a party,
and my step-father, Hugo Hasselbalch,
at the Tir aux Pigeons in Paris. He
taught me to shoot and gave me my
first shotgun.

Confirmed at thirteen, I had my picture taken as I was "no longer a child but a young lady."

The plump, quite Americanized coed at University of Southern California in 1951 was I!

At age eighteen, there were always lots of formal balls and weekend parties.

My second home, Piniehøj by the sea, owned by Hugo Hasselbalch.

Triumphant return to Copenhagen for a gala after success in Stockholm. Fees were small, though, as the costumes bear out!

One of the first publicity shots done in Geneva of Frederik and me, in June, 1957.

Frederik and I watching a charity football match—Copenhagen, 1958

Frederik and I attended the Moscow Film Festival in 1959.

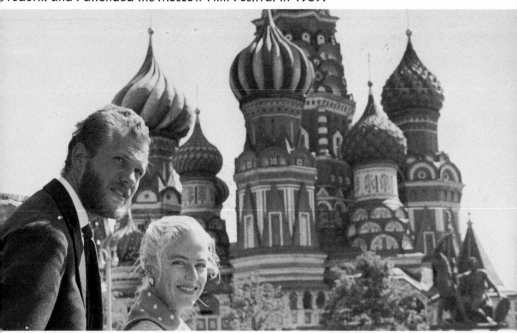

Our second movie, "The Melody of Love," with Louis Armstrong, 1959.

The house we owned for two months in Denmark, in 1961. Nicolas is in the pram.

he Ed Sullivan Show in December, 1961, the only performance we ever did to-
ether in the U.S.

My wedding day, September 21, 1960. Left to right: Frederik, my mother, Frederik's father and mother

Three generations of van Pallandts, Nicolas being the last male of this line of the family; Frederik, Nicolas, and Baron Floris van Pallandt

We did "Talk of The Town" in '64.

London, May 1966, with Nicolas, Kirsa and Ana Maria.

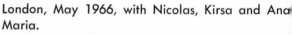

Frederik and I on a brief holiday in Ibiza, 1966.

e whole family in London, 1968.

During a Danish TV special, a bee was caught under my
dress and was busy stinging me on the left breast. . . .
But, the show must go on!

Frederik poring over navigational charts for his trip around worl

In concert at Royal Albert Hall, London, in spring of '69.

oing an hilarious cockney song in guest
ppearance on Max Bygrave's TV spe-
al, the show I've most enjoyed doing
nce working alone.

A TV show of my own for Thames Television.

First publicity shot as a soloist, done by Danish photographer friend, Svend Munk.

Another first publicity shot taken in Geneva, 1957.

uesting on a TV show in London, 1970.

At a German film premiere for most forgettable film I've ever seen, but it gave us three weeks on location in Venice.

Family picture of me in London 1962.

London, September 1971: before the storm

Not a modern-day Tarzan and Jane, but Elliott Goul◆ one of my co-stars (Sterling Hayden's the other) in "Th Long Goodbye," and I on location.

On the Malibu set of "The Long Goodbye," my first American film, with directo◆ Robert Altman and set visitor Sally Kellerman, who starred in an earlier Altma◆ movie, "M.A.S.H."

vided me with the latest gossip spiced with the internationally known names of jet-setting non-payers. *Very* interesting . . .

Charles spoke very little English and I was still bumbling along in French, but after a few weeks I was charmed out of my shoes and madly in love, prepared to wait forever . . . and I did. In June his mother died after a long illness of cancer, and the entire family went into its traditional year of formal mourning. One did not socialize or go anywhere. On several occasions when I hadn't heard from him, I took the Métro out to Père Lachaise Cemetery where his mother was buried, to put flowers on her grave. Things the lovelorn go through. . . .

I would now and then be invited for lunch or dinner at his home, always a frightening experience. My French being so limited, I felt incredibly stupid not being able to take part in the spirited and stimulating conversations. In this aristocratic home, I always felt like "la petite danoise" who lived somewhere in Paris on her own and didn't really belong in their circumstances. This was never said, of course, or even hinted at—I always received the most gracious hospitality—but it was something I sensed.

Classes ended and I returned home to Copenhagen for the summer holidays. Beyond the usual tennis, swimming and seeing old friends and family, little was memorable of those months except my stepfather's surprising me with a beautiful shotgun for my birthday. And, of couse, there were the many solitary hours daydreaming about Charles.

When I returned to Paris in the fall I found I had tired of the family scene on Rue de Saxe and found lodgings in the Hotel Chateaubriand on Rue de Cirque, a narrow street between Faubourg and the Champs Élysée—Right Bank, please note! It was not quite "down and out" in Paris, but close enough. My room was walk-in closet size with a single bulb hanging from the ceiling and facing onto a five-by-four foot shaft. Never being able to see the sky, I would mistake the drip-drip of the laundry hanging in the shaft for rain as it hit the tin rubbish bins at the bottom, and then I'd go haring out with rubber boots and mac—only to find the sun shining brightly.

The hotel was owned by a Mme. Brosse, but most of my dealings were with Mme. Cécile, the concierge who fast became my self-appointed protectress. A typical tiny land-lady in her seventies, she wore long dresses from another era, round steel-rimmed spectacles and an always uncombed mop of white hair. Her particular concern was screening my friends. Phone messages were relayed through the air shaft, and I could always tell from the tone of her voice whether she approved of the caller or not. She was an incorrigible snob and evaluated them instantly by the tone of voice, grammar and accent, taking it upon herself to say I was out if she disapproved. Needless to say, an aristocratic Frenchman with a chauffeured car was comparable in her eyes to winning the National Lottery! I frequently had to awaken her to get in if I arrived after 1:00 A.M. But again, her degree of cheer depended heavily on whom I'd been out with.

One day I had lunch with an old friend, the First Secretary of the Italian Embassy in Copenhagen. As a joke, he presented me with a box containing a two-inch live turtle with the name "Toto" painted on its back, a "roommate" of sorts to keep me from getting too lonely. After learning he was a land turtle, I made a home for him in the portable bidet in my room. Toto's eating habits—bits of lettuce, mostly—certainly didn't cut into my still strict budget. In fact, I often used to snitch the lettuce garnish from my dinner plate and store it until needed in a bag outside my window, next to my white wine.

Charles and I managed to sneak out to dinner in very dark, out-of-the way places or luncheons in country inns outside Paris. More likely than not, though, I'd end up in my room alone sipping wine, strumming my guitar and singing dolorous love songs to Toto by the light of one candle stuck into an old wine bottle. There is no place in the world like Paris for wallowing in the joys and miseries of an uncertain romance. I would wait days and weeks for a phone call, not daring to stir for fear he would miss me. Everything and everyone else were secondary. He seemed happy and content

98

when we were together, although he never made a direct declaration of love. I loved him so much I could make no demands—my love was enough for both of us. Most of my savings went for his Christmas and birthday presents and other little things, which I would buy at Hermés, way out of my price range but very much his style. The presents weren't large but were certainly selected with love.

In truth, my life was not quite so monastic as the above might lead one to believe. My French was progressing rapidly beyond the *la plume de ma tante* stage. After classes, everyone (mostly Americans and Canadians, as before) would drift into the cafés to gossip and solve the world's pressing problems over much coffee and *vin ordinaire,* or go in groups to exhibitions and museums. I was also getting out of my existentialist stage somewhat, spending some of my leftover funds each month on regular shoes instead of the usual sneakers, and accepting more invitations to formal dinners and balls. My artist and student friends never knew of my leading a double life socially. If I had a date for a ball with *Tout Paris,* I'd just tell them I was going out that evening, stroll casually out of Café Flor or wherever, then dash home to get out of my baggy pants and into my finery in time to be collected by a chauffeured car. At the end of a glamorous evening, quite like Cinderella, I'd return to my crummy hotel, get out of my formal gear and talk of the evening's happenings to Toto, asleep in his bidet. I rather enjoyed that dual existence and frequently preferred the company at Deux Magots to what would eventually be labeled the "Jet Set." It always amused me to carry my favorite white organdy gown in a huge bag under my black-sweatered arm to the best hand laundry in Paris to have it starched and done up for the next big event. Many times while walking through my neighborhood, I'd see my two *clochards,* whose friendship I greatly cherished. *Clochards* are old winos or hobos who sit on the banks of the Seine or huddle over Métro gratings in the winter to keep warm. These two preferred a particular bench on the Champs Élysée right around the corner from the Châteaubriand. Whenever I came down the street, one always got up, bowed very deeply

99

and swept his battered old hat to the pavement. He used to call me his "ray of sunshine." I'd curtsy quite formally in response (not easy in black pants and sneakers), then we'd both do a little dance right there with half the traffic of Paris whizzing by.

Sometimes I'd sneak out late after studying most of the evening, and head for one of the late-night cafés in the area. There, with a mug of hot cocoa and a piece of baguette with butter, I'd sit for hours, completely enthralled by the night people: pimps, prostitutes, showgirls, roués-at-large making their last rounds of the evening. It was a wildly different world, and no one ever bothered me as I fascinatedly took it all in. Sometimes I got into conversations . . . and really believed I was studying life.

Not all my life was spent gaping at showgirls or singing to myself. There were lots of young men I'd met in classes or through friends, and we'd take in several of our crowd's favorite spots. If a date were well-heeled, there'd be Jimmy's, a very popular nightclub. Most of the students preferred the various Saint Germain cafés, La Rose Rouge on the Left Bank and our pet stand-by, Deux Magots. One of my favorites was L'Abbaye, a small cabaret, where two American guys, one black, one white, sang and played guitars. That was my first introduction to folk-singing in a commercial sense, and I still own and play their records.

On one of my stepfather's visits to Paris, he met the two *clochards* as we were walking to lunch at Fouquet's, and was quite amused. He also introduced me to one of the most colorful personalities ever, whom unbeknownst to him, I called "Mon Oncle." He was from one of France's old and illustrious families, married and with children, but he and his wife lived in separate villas side-by-side in one of the most fashionable parts of Paris. They visited back and forth through a hole in the hedge between the two houses, but each conducted his own life and affairs quite separately—very French, indeed!

He was the complete aesthete, with impeccable taste and style. His villa, the antiques, the paintings, the boiserie, the library of rare books, the food and the wine—everything was exquisite. His dinners were not unlike the salons of earlier centuries, all beautiful women and brilliant men. When I looked about at the women there, my guess was that most had been, were or would soon be one of his mistresses. The conversation was highly intellectual and very *spirituel,* the men being politicians, writers, high-powered businessmen and generally in influential positions. "Mon Oncle" became a sort of confidant, since he was one of the few people who knew of my somewhat unrequited love for Charles.

"Mon Oncle" also had a beautiful shooting lodge in Alsace, to which I was invited for a boar and stag hunt, and flew there in the private plane of the Bao Dai, Emperor of Indochina. The ambiance of Paris was transferred on a small scale—again feminine beauty and male brilliance were much in evidence, the one condition being that you could shoot. Every room in the house had a game-oriented name and motif on walls, curtains and knick-knacks. Dinner was formal attire, and I never saw the same table service twice, though the designs on linens, china and crystal always had something to do with hunting.

Before drinks one evening, I met my host in the hallway. "Come here," he said, "I want to show you something." He gestured toward a wall of old-fashioned flower prints, which I'd passed a dozen times already. But, as I looked at them closely, I found the flowers were really people making love in every conceivable and inconceivable position, quite like the caves of Ilora. As if I weren't embarrassed enough, he then pulled open one of the pictures, which was actually a little door, to reveal one of the guests, a beautiful, well-known model, stretched out in all her naked splendor in the bathtub. I blushed noticeably and my friend roared with laughter, then escorted me downstairs for a much-needed drink. That night, I made a careful check of all pictures and mirrors in bedroom and bath before going to sleep.

As the spring term rolled on and my rendezvous with Charles were no less sporadic than before, I decided to take a holiday from it all. Easter was coming up and many of my

101

student friends were talking about Majorca—informal, sunny and very cheap—just what I needed.

I took the third-class train from Paris to Barcelona, where I boarded the overnight boat to Majorca. My deck accommodations (the very cheapest available) found me sharing space with one hundred and fifty Majorcan soldiers on leave. I quickly sidled up to the few non-Spanish-looking youths near me and, feeling rather protected, readied myself to bed down on deck with knapsack and guitar. It was a full moon, though, and wine was being passed around. Other guitars appeared, and little by little, an all-night concert was underway using the hatch cover as our impromptu stage. We all joined in, and it was an incredible night. Everyone was very bleary-eyed when we reached Palma at six the next morning, and I still had to travel by bus to Puerto Soller and my hotel on the beach. The second day I decided to explore some of the island by motor scooter. I do think the manager of the scooter rental agency suspected I had never ridden one before, despite my protestations to the contrary, for he very chivalrously started the machine for me, helped me on, and let go. In less than a minute I found my scooter wheels stuck in the tram tracks running down the middle of the main street. Coming to a bend in the tracks, I tried to get out of my rut in the literal sense of the word, but instead sailed head over heels right into the center of the village square. Fortunately, no harm was done and the scooter was undamaged. More embarrassing than the flop was the fact that I really *didn't* know how to start it and had to drag it into a narrow side street to figure the damn thing out in secret.

All told, there were about ten students of various nationalities from the university trickling into the hotel, so the entire week was a marvelous international party. Majorca then was totally untouched by the ravages of tourism, and was still primitive. The sea was clean and crystal clear, the mode of transportation mainly horse and cart, the beaches deserted. The towns had the timeless dreamy drowsiness of southern Europe. I went everywhere on my scooter and saw the whole island. Since then I have been back twice, only to work there, never wanting to see the devastation tourism has wreaked.

The trip back to Paris was not so festive. The weather during the voyage from Majorca to Barcelona was terrible. Three of us had booked deck space again, but four others had gotten a second class room with bunk beds. Sometime in the middle of the night, the storm and the rough seas became so bad, and sleep was not helped by a man next to me constantly tapping his wooden leg on the deck, that we invaded our friends' cabin. There we were, seven of us in four bunks in steerage, one of the foulest smelling places I've ever survived; all pretending we weren't feeling deathly ill. The next morning we pooled our funds and took a room in Barcelona just to wash off the grub and the stink, and by late afternoon, were back on the train for Paris, all sound asleep.

Shortly after my return, Mother, Sussi and I were dining in Paris and noticed a rather dissipated-looking but still handsome man talking animatedly in the corner. Poking my mother, I hissed: "Look, there's Errol Flynn, the movie actor." She looked at the sagging jowls and paunchy physique and told me I was wrong. We paid our check and left. As we were standing in the middle of the Boulevard trying to find a cab, our elbows were grasped by two masculine hands. Then that unmistakable voice, which even convinced Mother, said: "Really, you ladies shouldn't be standing in the middle of the street . . . you'll be run over. You must let me drop you at your hotel. . . ." No sooner said than done—his limousine drove up and before we could protest, politely, of course, we were off to Mother's hotel. He was devastatingly charming and Mother confessed to having been picked up in the street for the very first time in her life.

The next day he sent a note to my mother requesting her permission to take me to lunch the following day. Captivated by his old-world courtliness and totally ignorant of his rakish reputation, which had received little press in Denmark, she replied that I'd be delighted—and of course, I was. We went to a quaint but very good little restaurant and talked, he doing most of the talking. He asked if I had ever acted, if I'd ever been a model and, finally, if I'd be interested in testing for a part in his next movie.

I was both flattered and flustered. He then added that the

103

part involved nude scenes and that he would, therefore, have to see what I looked like without clothes—purely for professional reasons, he assured me with a look that was entirely unprofessional. I told him I didn't think I was quite ready for the career he had in mind, and lunch came to a rather quick finish. But what a charmer he was.

Summer was nearing, exams were coming up at the Alliance Française, and classmates were already discussing where they'd go next. Charles was now back in circulation and taking part in all the parties and balls of *Tout Paris*. Although we danced and chatted at the same parties, Rubirosa and Aly Khan had nothing on Charles in my eyes. But I had now begun moving from the world of daydreams—could he only have known the exploits and adventures we shared in my imagination!—to the world of cold reality. He was French and a Catholic, I a Protestant Dane; his name old and illustrious, mine. . . . All the traditional barriers—and I still didn't *really* know how he felt about me.

Having suffered from this unrest for months, I finally finished exams, took leave of Charles and my friends, gave Toto to Mme. Cécile (who didn't seem particularly pleased), packed up guitar, shotgun, eiderdown and other paraphernalia and got on the third class going North.

I'd been cured of my longing for America long since, but now I was smitten by Paris. And I was miserable . . . again.

Senora Wessel

No matter how confused my state of mind, to
arrive home at Midsummer with the garden in
full bloom and no hours of darkness whatsoever has always
restored my sense of "earth roots" and mellowed my sadness
of the moment. As usual, I found the house full of life. St.
Hans Eve preparations were in the works. The legend is that
on that night all the witches go off to Bloksbjerg for their
annual gathering, and everyone lights huge bonfires on the
beach with a scarecrow-type witch on top. We often stuck
rockets and firecrackers onto her broomstick to speed her on
her journey. Then we'd drive up and down the coast visiting
friends—everyone has open house with big punch bowls of
white wine and fresh fruits.

All night at that time of year, there is the pink-yellow glow
of a perpetual sunset in the sky and the hush of expectancy in
the air. No one goes to bed, and even the birds stop singing
for only an hour or so. It's as though all of nature and all the
people are emerging from the great cocoon of winter's darkness, drinking in the whole phenomenon with heady awe.
Scandinavians who have moved away from that part of the
world are always most homesick for that experience. Maybe
it's a throwback to our pagan forebears and their worship of

the sun—what other aspect of nature could be more revered than that which brings light and life after those black and dormant winters?

This particular summer the usual beehive of activity and house guests was greatly accelerated by Mother's preparations for my sister's wedding in August. In all the whirl, I felt a bit out of it and in more than a bit of a quandary about my own life. There was great solace in walking miles up and down the beach at night. As always, the sea had its soothing effect on my inner turmoil, although the problems were still with me.

Among the guests arriving that summer was Hugo Wessel, and he was a most welcome sight. He'd long been taken in as a son at Piniehøj, my stepfather/godfather being his godfather, too. His own father had died several years before and his mother, whom he'd only just met again (his parents had been divorced when he was a baby, and he was brought up in America by his father), was living in England with her third husband.

My mother undoubtedly has the biggest "mother's bosom" in all of Denmark. There was always room for one more "son" or "daughter," and to this flock she had added Hugo. To this day, her house is always filled with young people who seek her out. She's the only one I know whose calendar of birthday cards and gifts increases enormously year after year—by now, it must include three generations, and maybe four.

That summer Hugo became my constant companion. We went everywhere together, did everything together, and our college romance in California underwent a renaissance. There were a few calls from Charles, but in all the flurry they somehow never reached me. I had gradually put him from my mind. Mother's consoling comment that "Frenchmen make totally unsatisfactory and unfaithful husbands" only confirmed the feeling that my decision was the right one: Hugo asked me to marry him and I said yes.

There have been certain decisions in my life that I have made impulsively—decisions that would gravely influence the rest of my life. These resolutions of rather ponderous situations have always crystallized in a flash: I just decide, come hell

106

or high water. Invariably, both hell and high water do come in wholesale lots.

Without telling anyone, he and I got all the necessary papers and forms together, then presented Mother with the *fait accompli.* She was speechless, one of the very few times she's ever been at a loss for words, for this meant she would have to get another wedding together in the two weeks left before Sussi's. Her recovery to her cool, very organized self was instant, though. "Oh, children!" she exulted and happily began planning the hundreds of details.

Sussi was having an old-fashioned Danish wedding dinner; I would be married in the same local church with a formal afternoon garden reception two days before. Guest lists were immediately drawn. Actually, most of the relatives, old friends and other guests planning to attend Sussi's would already be on hand for mine, which greatly simplified matters. A striped tent and flowers were ordered, caterers given their near-impossible assignments, hundreds of tiny gilt chairs rented and my wedding gown planned. For that we turned to "Bette with the gentle smile," the seamstress who'd reigned supreme in our sewing room for years making all our ball gowns. Although she was already busy with Sussi's gown, she turned to the yards and yards of white tulle without hesitation and produced yet another creation of simplicity and loveliness. In the midst of all this, we tore all over Copenhagen buying my household trousseau: pots and pans, china, crystal, stainless steel, linens—everything. In this incredible pile of stuff were 124 Irish linen dish towels, without which Mother was convinced I could not run a home properly. At last check, there were still two of them, unused, in my linen drawer!

Hugo's mother as well as his stepmother arrived a few days before the ceremony. Helen Lee, Hugo's stepmother, was a wealthy American who had been his father's last wife and now lived in Chile. She had not had any children in her marriages and had taken Hugo under her wing as her protegé. At the time of our marriage, Hugo had a degeee in liberal arts from Occidental but no plans for a career at all, so it was easy for Helen to persuade us to live with her in Santiago. She was very active in Chilean philanthropies and the international social life of the capital, and would introduce Hugo to the right people, get him set in a good position and make him her heir.

Two nights before my wedding, Mother solemnly called me into her bedroom for her collection of prenuptial advice. Of all of it, I most remember: "You must always keep in mind the closed bathroom door policy. Don't ever let your husband see you first thing in the morning. Be sure you have been to the bathroom, washed, brushed your teeth and put a pink bow in your hair. And, don't ever let him catch you sitting on the loo!" I suppose that's one way of holding on to your illusions!

Just before leaving for the church, an incident took place which, in sheer excitement, practically overshadowed everything else. Mother couldn't find the key to the cupboard in which she kept the key for the drawer in which she kept the key for the safe in which her jewelry was stored. The alarm was sent out for valet, nanny, maids and all, and the treasure hunt in my mother's bedroom began, not ending until seven minutes before the ceremony. Happily, key and jewels were found, last-minute instructions given to the staff, kisses blown to those staying behind—and we were off.

Through the superhuman efforts of Mother and the staff plus a gift from the gods of glorious weather, the wedding went beautifully. The reception was perfect: a sumptuous buffet, an unceasing flow of champagne, much dancing and the fun of seeing old friends. To break up the party, Hugo and I obviously had to leave. But, in the mad dash between "engagement" and altar, we'd completely forgotten to plan a proper honeymoon! Firmly urged on by my mother, however, we took off for a small hotel in Elsinore amidst a shower of rice—with but one toothbrush between us! Quite honestly, we hadn't wanted to leave the comforts of home at all—and were back at nine the next morning in time for tea and toast.

The Wessel family, with all its marriages, half-siblings, stepparents and history, was a fascinating one. Hugo's father, Tito Wessel, was one of four extraordinary and very wealthy Danish brothers. He was a true gentleman of leisure with a flair for enjoying it. When he was married to Hugo's mother, he had installed a grand piano for her on his large yacht, *The White Shadow*. They'd sailed much of the world on it, spending a good deal of their time on Moorea, a small island of which he owned half just off Tahiti. Years later, Hugo and his sisters sold it for only $50,000 to a butcher from San Francisco. At least that's the story I heard.

Hugo's mother was unlike any one I've ever met, the true eccentric Englishwoman, regal in manner and extremely witty. One could not help but admire and love her. Born Denise Orme but nicknamed Jo, she had briefly been on the stage and then married Lord Churston, with whom she had several children.

Her second marriage was to Tito Wessel, by whom she had Hugo at the tender age of forty-eight or fifty—no one really knew her age, for it had always been tinkered with in her passport. Their marriage ended in divorce, and her third marriage was to the Duke of Leinster.

Once she took me to Woburn Abbey, the seat of the Dukes of Bedford, to see its beautiful treasures and to meet some of her family (Hugo's half-sister had become Duchess of Bedford). Jo first led me through rooms of silver—bowls, goblets, tureens, flatware, huge candelabra and epergnes, trays large enough to carry a roasted boar, a dazzling array. Then she went on to more rooms equally stuffed with the same sort of things—but all in gold vermeil. I was still agog as she turned to me and said, "The silver is quite beautiful, but frankly, I do prefer the gold—you don't have to polish it."

Once near her home in Jersey, so the story goes, on a day when the Army were out on maneuvers nearby, Jo drove round a bend on a country road and ran into a parked jeep, heavily camouflaged with leaves and branches. When the soldier leapt out and remonstrated with her, she replied innocently, "I *thought* I wasn't supposed to see you."

Hugo and I had my household trousseau packed into scores of crates for shipment by sea and got ourselves and our clothing onto a plane for Santiago within a week after Sussi's marriage. By then, she was on her honeymoon, but we'd already said our goodbyes, unhappy we'd be living so far from each other. Although we hadn't seen much of each other over the past several years, Sussi being the homebody and I, of course, ever flying to the four winds, there still was the closeness of having shared so much together. I would miss her.

When Hugo and I arrived at Helen Lee's beautiful hacienda in the foothills outside Santiago, she was off on an extended honeymoon with a Danish family friend she'd married unexpectedly a week after our wedding. The hacienda was a collection of four connected buildings set at right angles around a lovely courtyard and entered through a magnificent wrought-iron gate. The household and a pack of yapping dogs were all watched over by the Chilean caretaker and his wife. My first few weeks at Helen Lee's were exhausting, not from physical work but rather the language barrier and nothing to do. The staff spoke no English, I was just learning Spanish and our sign language exercises had me worn out by lunchtime. To alleviate the loneliness and silence, I used to walk around that square house, first right to left, then left to right. I also played the old gramaphone when things really got desperate. "His Master's Voice" never quite came to more than a truce with its transformer, and Enrico Caruso sounded more like Donald Duck—but anything to break the monotony.

Hugo and I used to dine *à deux* in a large dining room at opposite ends of an enormous table, rather like a cozy evening at Hearst Castle. I several times thought of installing telephones at either end, though I doubt our communication would have been much better anyway.

Hugo took a job, the first he'd ever had (and the last as far as I know). He worked diligently for the Grace Lines for two months, pronounced the whole thing "a goddamn bore" and retired to the leisurely life of detective novels and Scrabble. Despite what would become his permanent absence from the rolls of the employed, he was not penniless. Under the guardianship of his late father's banker, there was a comfortable inheritance which, while not permitting great extravagance, allowed him to live quite well. In the meantime, I was recovering from a galloping case of dysentery caused, I found, by drinking water containing a large quantity of untreated sewage.

After the doctor had diagnosed my problem, he sent around *el Practicante* to give me the shots I needed to get rid of the affliction. In came a thin, shifty-eyed character wearing a greasy pin-striped suit and too-tight tie, and displaying the longest, dirtiest fingernails I'd ever seen. He toted a handful of rusty hypodermics, and nervously explained that he usually gave shots only to sick animals but was the only *Practicante* on duty in that district. I felt sorry for the dogs and sheep! Invariably he'd hit the nerves in my bottom so badly that my toes would stand out from my feet like the points of a star and stay that way for at least three hours after his departure! My health and my Spanish improved simultaneously.

The coming of Christmas was made official by the arrival of Helen Lee and her new husband. It took no time for me to see that two new marriages under one roof would not work, but Hugo had been in no hurry to find a home of our own. The tension mounted, and a few nights after Christmas, Hugo came to me in a terrible state, said we weren't wanted there anymore and were getting out right away. I tried to get him to tell me what had happened, but he refused. It was a forty-five minute drive into town, but we had no car except for the one we'd been borrowing from the household. I took one look at my personal belongings and wondered how on earth I was going to truck all of them out of there on foot. I decided the first thing I'd transport would be myself—the suitcases could always be fetched—threw a toothbrush into my handbag and started traipsing down the road. No one was going to tell *me* I was unwelcome, nor was there any way I was going to stay there five minutes longer.

I can't recall Hugo's method of transportation, but we each headed for our half-finished unheated house down the road a mile or two and spent the night sleeping in our overcoats on the floor. The next day we moved the rest of our things, and for the next several months camped out in that shell of a house, never really settling in. We did get curtains and a few odd bits and pieces to make it liveable, but all the major household gear was still in transit from Denmark and didn't arrive until we were almost ready to leave Chile altogether.

We'd already met many prominent Chileans and foreigners

and entertained them in our modest way. Our house was situated in a group of half-completed semi-detached homes, and all around were empty lots cluttered with the crude shacks the workmen had thrown up for their families. Fridays I remember most vividly: that was pay day, a good time to keep off the nearby streets. The workers would invariably spend most of their money on liquor, have noisy brawls often ending in bloodshed, then be dragged home by their wives as their children watched cowering in the background. In the early frosty winter mornings when I used to drive to the market, I'd see dozens of little kids, mostly orphans, foraging through the garbage pails of the rich residential areas. Then, huddled in their tatters over little fires built on the spot, they would heat their finds in old tincans. These urchins were all alone in the world, save for each other. One lady started a shelter for them, but all she could offer was a warm, dry place to sleep. Come dawn, they'd all be in the streets again hunting for food or helping carry baskets in the markets for a penny or two. It was my first day-to-day living with abject poverty and it haunted me long after I left there.

Having grown up in a highly efficient welfare state where poverty was hardly known and everyone was assured of decent food, housing and medical care, these conditions appalled me, and the contrast of the wealth of the Catholic Church was striking. Once, in a particularly opulent cathedral, I asked a peasant how it was that his church had so much while he had so little. He seemed surprised and even shocked as though no one had ever considered such a thing, then looked about him with pride and said: "But, Senora, this all belongs to us."

Helen Lee donated to the local parish a Ford station wagon, worth at least ten to twelve thousand dollars on the black market, to be raffled off for the church emergency relief fund. Two months later, the rotund priest paid her a visit, and much to our surprise was driving the same wagon. His reply to our question about it was, "My flock felt I needed it to get around." Considering that his flock consisted of the poorest people in Santiago, living in mud huts in a dried-up river bed, his explanation was not totally satisfactory.

It didn't take long for me to discover that Hugo, while sweet and kind, was rather tight. To meet our quite simple household expenses and to avoid scenes, I used to pinch money out of his pockets while he was asleep and began selling my clothes at a second-hand shop run by an American friend. From this American friend, we also got most of the local gossip, especially about the ingenuity used by government officials and private individuals to defraud the government itself.

There were tremendous import taxes on almost all consumer goods, but one man in the retail shoe business figured it all out. He would have all the left feet shipped in through a northern free port, and all the right feet in through Valparaiso. Since in that state the shoes were useless, he paid no tax, but later had the pairs mated properly in Santiago.

An American friend of ours who was the top sales representative of a major automotive plant in the States was trying to sell public buses to the Chilean government. Everything was agreed upon until it came to price. He quoted a figure of about $18,000 per bus. The official of the transportation ministry agreed, but told him the bills were to be made out for $24,000 per bus. Our friend replied in the usual polite circumlocution of such cases that there was no way he could comply with this scheme. We later heard the contract went to the Japanese.

The most hilarious of all the hundreds of such stories we heard was the one about the army colonel who made a killing in the automobile business. There was a great market for foreign cars in Chile, but an astronomical tax on them unless one was a citizen. However, the colonel was well-versed in a little-known law stating that a Chilean citizen who had lived outside the country for more than five years could bring in a car and pay no tax at all. Now, it so happened that most of the successful ladies of easy virtue in Buenos Aires were, in fact, Chileans. He made a fast trip to Argentina and made the following proposition to the girls: He would secretly put up the money for them to buy new cars which they would then turn over to him. In return, they would receive a small per-

113

centage of the profits made on his reselling the vehicles in Chile, plus a free round trip and two-week holiday at Santiago's most expensive hotel. One of the highlights of Santiago's social life at that time would be to sit on the terrace of that hotel and watch the girls cavort at the pool below.

Most of the social scene in Santiago revolved around dinners and parties in private homes. For us the big after-dinner diversion was Scrabble, which we played incessantly, but good as it was for my vocabulary, it was not doing much to help our marriage.

A welcome respite from town living were the weekends at the ranch home of a Chilean friend. Maria Louisa was a complete nature-child. (When she was about seven-and-a-half months pregnant, she fell out of a tree and delivered prematurely but safely. I still haven't the foggiest notion what she was doing up there in the first place.)

She and I used to get up at 4:00 A.M., when the stars were still out, the frost still on the ground and the air very crisp. We'd wrap ourselves in huge black ponchos and creep out to the stables to awaken the stable boy in his oatsbin bed that looked just like an old coffin. He'd saddle up two of the small short-gaited horses, which are specially bred to climb up and, hopefully, back down steep mountain sides without mishap. The saddles were sheepskins, from which hung stirrups that looked like the front ends of wooden shoes. Off we'd go, charging up the mountain to reach the peak just at sunrise and watch the blanket of clouds covering the valleys below slowly rise and dissolve. Then we'd ride all day, having a lunch of wild mushrooms which the locals never touched, presumably not knowing what they were . . . neither did we, as far as their being safe or poisonous was concerned, but relying on blind faith and empty stomachs, we'd fill our scarves, bundle them up and roast them over an open fire.

Sometimes we'd spot an innocent shepherd in the distance and race off in the opposite direction, as if he were after us— our own version of cowboys and Indians. I'm sure the sight of two women, hair and black capes flying as they tore across the mountaintops on horseback, drove many of the locals right into their churches.

114

One day we heard that some of the Indian farmworkers at Maria Louisa's place were having a wake. A newborn baby in their community had died and, as was their custom, they were about to crucify it on a wall of its parents' hut. Their belief was that the newborn child's spirit was so pure that its soul would go directly to Heaven and, thus, could carry their wants and wishes straight to God. This was completely different from any view of death I'd ever known, but as curious as we were to attend, we decided against going so as not to intrude.

It was about that time that I got my dog, Osorio. Friends of ours—the husband was the head of a government department—had seven children and eleven dogs, and the fruits of his job were equally obvious: four or five new cars, several hi-fi sets, washing machines, appliances of all sorts. The last of the eleven dogs, a black almost-pure Alsatian with huge soulful amber eyes, took an instant liking to me. In my own unsubtle way (and since the dog looked as though he wasn't getting much attention), I indicated I wouldn't mind relieving them of one of their many responsibilities. Two hours later he was perched next to me in my car, riding home.

Around mid-June—we'd been in Santiago since the previous September—my household gear arrived from Denmark. By that time, Hugo and I were growing rapidly apart. I was finding our lack of a meaningful existence increasingly frustrating, and there was a total lack of communication between us. Life in Santiago was stagnating—food, drink and Scrabble weren't exactly my idea of living. We talked of going to California, to Santa Barbara where Hugo's father had once owned a home. However, I would first have to return to Denmark, apply for immigration papers and wait for my turn, the Danish quota for America being very small and always filled. Hugo had kept his Danish nationality but already had his residency, so he could go directly. Therefore, we divided the trousseau into two lots: antiques from my mother, some special wedding presents and my paperweight collection would go directly to friends of his in Santa Barbara for storage. The bulk of the household gear I insisted on selling right there in Santiago to pay, first of all, for Osorio's plane ticket home to Copenhagen and then our fares, too. Hugo didn't especially approve of the sale, but at this point I found my economic freedom far more important than crates full of possessions. Besides, *he* wasn't about to pay for Osorio's plane ticket. I put a notice in the paper, not giving my name but merely the address, made a beautiful shop-like display of glass, china, stainless steel, crockery, pots and pans, linen and all, and sat down and waited. The open house was to be between 7:00 and 9:00 P.M. Hugo had fled the humiliating scene much earlier and, as I sat there with my ledger sheet, my courage sank. The prices I had put on everything were quite outrageous except for the fact that imported things were very scarce and practically unobtainable in Chile at that time. If available, they'd be as outrageously priced as mine. Came eight o'clock, Osorio and I were still holding each other's hand and paw, when suddenly a knock came on the door. In walked two generations of one of the most prominent Chilean families, all of whom I knew quite well. I kept a straight face and, within half an hour, the house was full of the social blue book of Santiago. They, too, kept straight faces at the sight of the prices, and business was brisk.

I thought I would die of embarrassment but all the customers seemed to be pleased with their finds. Of course it had to happen that night that the electricity was cut. As if my shameless prices weren't bad enough, the situation was magnified a hundredfold by my customers having to ask me to read the price tags in the flickering light of the candles.

That same light undoubtedly covered my blushing. Came midnight, Osorio and I sat in an almost empty house congratulating each other upon our mercenary exploits. Came one o'clock, Hugo returned to find me triumphantly waving a shoebox overflowing with money and checks—Osorio was assured of his fare.

I cabled my mother and followed up with a letter, the first mail she'd had from me in some time, since there hadn't been much good news to report, and I wasn't about to dump my unhappiness into her long-distance lap. My instructions regarding Osorio were that she was to take with her to the airport a piece of my clothing plus lots of hamburger and pâté. She later told me she'd immediately collected the stuff and then, one midnight, got a call from the airport. There was a huge beast in a crate out there, and would she *please* come out and sign a receipt for it so it could be shipped to the mandatory quarantine kennels. When the cargo men opened the crate, the "beast" tore out, picked up the scent of the food and my Zahles graduation cap, and jumped up with both his front paws on my mother's shoulders. She nearly fainted—after all, Osorio weighed 125 pounds. Although she was never much of an animal lover, Mother faithfully visited him every day for his six weeks of quarantine, bringing him ground meat and sausages and wearing her special Osorio smock. She grew to love and adore him and had him for nearly eight years. During my stepfather's illness and afterward in her flat in Copenhagen, she and Osorio used to sit watching TV together, sound asleep! Eventually, a situation occurred which indicates how incredibly mean people can be. Osorio was quite old and not very well, though still a gentle, quiet and clean dog. Some people in one of the other flats wanted to get a poodle but were told that pets were not permitted. They objected, pointing out that my mother had a dog. She, however, explained that she had had Osorio for eight years, he was nearly on his last legs, and could not be given away. Another nasty neighbor joined the argument. Despite my mother's pleadings, the neighbors insisted on their equal rights. The outcome was *nobody* was allowed pets—she had to have him put away. For months after, hamburgers and hot dogs were banned from the table, as none of us could look at them, let alone eat them.

With the dog safely off to Denmark, I then turned to the settling of my own affairs. With money from the sale of my trousseau, I bought a one-way boat ticket to Copenhagen while Hugo took off for California. I hated leaving the beautiful countryside and the mountains, where I'd spent so many happy hours, and I would miss the friends I'd made, but otherwise Chile held nothing for me.

On the ship, I had ample time to reflect upon our marriage and what had gone wrong. Trying to revive love and romance from other days and other places is always precarious, and believing that geographical displacement would be a help was a complete fallacy. When Hugo had returned to Piniehøj the preceding summer, the family's encouragement, overt and otherwise, had made our getting together such an easy, natural extension of lifelong security and tradition. When this extension did not continue in Chile, things fell apart. There, no longer children of the house, we were left to our own devices, and we had no devices in common.

"Nina and Frederik"

My mother knew I was troubled but never pried into my thoughts. She knew I had to wait for my immigration visa for a long while, maybe long enough to sort things out in my own mind. Still feeling under parental authority and afraid to tell anyone, especially her, that I'd already resolved not to go to California, I began looking for occupational therapy, both to distract me from myself and to earn some money.

I'd noticed the great fascination Americans had for beaded clothing, formal or informal. Scrounging around Haandar-bejdds Fremme, a beautiful handicraft shop started in Copenhagen years before by an aunt of mine and her friends to promote and preserve traditional Danish craft and design, I found some bolts of handwoven wool. This particular flow-ered pattern was the one used for the most popular of the many regional national costumes. I bought enough of the material for a skirt, plus a sack of black beads which I began sewing into the middle of every flower. (It got to the point where I went to bed each night counting black dots instead of sheep.) Every corner of the house had traces of my handiwork, and wherever one sat one risked getting up with an intricate pattern of shiny crystals pasted to his rump. My first article for sale proved sewing was my forte, not retailing: I put 2,400 beads on a skirt in five days and got paid ten dollars.

More important than the money, though, was the inclusion of that first skirt in a crafts exhibit at the National Arts Museum in Copenhagen, an accomplishment that pleased and amused me no end, having flunked sewing classes all through school. One wouldn't think it possible to pass the winter beading night and day, but I did. I must have gotten to bead number 250,699 when the doorbell rang. It was Frederik— he'd walked down the beach to our place from his uncle's and was just back from New York.

I had always liked and secretly admired Frederik, and now he was more elegant than ever—very tall and graceful, copper-blond hair and beard, tan, and with those devastating blue eyes. He was very extroverted, had a marvelous sense of humor and an air of great self-confidence. Despite our being the same age, he always seemed much more worldly than I could ever hope to be.

His whole life, hopscotching about the world with his diplomat family, had fostered much of that. Born in The Netherlands, he had gone to prep schools in Washington, D.C., England and Switzerland, finally studying under a private tutor in Holland to obtain a secondary school diploma. At the beginning of World War II he was booked on a convoy from Portugal to America, but was stricken with appendicitis the night before departure and couldn't leave. Two days later, the convoy was sunk by a patrol of German U-boats. There were no survivors.

After high school, he lived with his parents for two years in India, where his father was the Dutch ambassador, then enrolled in the Tropical Agricultural College in Trinidad. After a year and a half in jungle exotica he moved on to McGill University in Montreal where he studied English literature, then to The New School of Social Research in Greenwich Village for a major in Russian literature. He's often laughed about his Russian literature classes there: it took him two months to figure out the lecture was in English, the professor's accent was so thick.

When Frederik and I met again that April, 1957, in Copenhagen, he'd just arrived for a long summer holiday. He'd brought his guitar and we began singing together, teaching each other folk songs we'd picked up in various parts of the world, he handling the melody, I the harmonizing. Our best place to practice was the huge cavernous kitchen with its marvelous acoustics. In the afternoons when it was deserted, we used to take over.

Frederik's mother had heard our folk doodlings and, one night after dinner, asked if we'd sing a couple of her favorites for the guests. A family friend said he knew a man in the impresario business in Copenhagen who was always looking for fresh new talent. Why didn't we give him a call?

"No!" said I.

"Oh, yes!" said Frederik. He won.

Frederik had always entertained the idea of performing professionally, possibly with a band of his own. He'd studied guitar briefly in Buenos Aires with a professor who would have been a concert guitarist except for the fact that he suffered from extremely painful hand cramping that came and went without warning, precluding his scheduling appearances. "The guitar is the most beautiful instrument, for it is the one you hold and play closest to the heart," was a saying of his which Frederik never forgot.

Frederik called the impresario, who arranged for an audition a few days later at the Mon Coeur cabaret in Tivoli. The entertainment there was directed by an expatriate Hungarian, Fritz Rutzika, and his Danish wife, Kate Rosén. They'd given many young poets, singers, comedians and musicians their first professional opportunity, and they too participated in the show as singers, and entertained the guests in informal table-hopping.

Our appointment was at 11:00 A.M. There is nothing dingier and less welcoming than a nightclub in bright daylight. Fritz greeted us brusquely. He seemed inattentive and didn't remove his camel's hair coat with the upturned collar or his large dark glasses. He was surprised to hear us sing, as he'd thought he'd be auditioning a dancing team. We stood on the

121

empty floor and performed to the accompaniment of vacuum cleaners, floor polishers and sleepy waiters muttering in the background, while the stench of stale booze and cigarettes permeated all. I looked down at the floor and Frederik stared holes into the ceiling as we sang the two or three songs we knew really well. It was dreadful. After a pause, "Ja, ja, learn more songs, come back in June to rehearse—you open July 1."

We couldn't believe it, even when we'd signed our contract for five dollars a night. I still don't know how much weight our singing talent then carried, but he surely saw the news value of "society goes on stage." When we got home, our families and friends all thought it splendid and enthusiastically began making plans for the opening. (I don't think Frederik's aristocratic forebears would ever have believed some of their twentieth century descendants would end up as "court jesters," but then *they* had the special privilege of minting their own coins, and their family estates were large and full of Dutch masters. They had been Dutch landholders for hundreds of years, serving monarchs back to William of Orange. Unfortunately, Frederik told me, some family members had tried to join "modern times" through stock investments, that is, the Russian Imperial Railway in 1916. Frederik's mother was born Countess Blücher-Altona, a descendant of the famous General Blücher.)

Frederik and I did the town that night to celebrate with congratulatory gifts of cash from my stepfather and his mother. We ran out of money at 4:00 A.M., and had to leave Frederik's gold cigarette case to pay our bill. The Pallandt family returned to Swtizerland, and I followed shortly after to spend a month in Geneva rehearsing with Frederik—and learning to enjoy curries. They were on the menu quite often, Frederik's sister Clara having learned to prepare the real thing in India. I'd eat mine with tears in my eyes, sweat pouring from my brow, convinced that any minute my tongue was going to fall out, yet politely nod approval over glass upon glass of water. For these dinners, we'd dress up in Clara's saris and feel very Indian and graceful.

That month also brought my introduction to Eastern mysti-

122

cism. Frederik's father, when a young man, had met Inayat Khan, who had brought the Sufi message from India to Europe in 1912. To sum up Sufism in a few words is impossible—it's a whole philosophy of life but . . . in Inayat Khan's words, "The way of a Sufi is to experience life and yet remain above it, to live in the world and not let the world own him." His world message was "Love, harmony and beauty." His nephew, Ali Khan (no relation to the Aga Khan) was then head of the movement, lived in Geneva and often visited the Pallandt home. Old, frail and completely blind, he still had an incredible aura about him—you couldn't help but feel his presence. There was an enveloping peace about him as he sat and talked parables—he never sermonized. He and Nora Élé transmitted the same inner strength, which I recognized and was awed by, of someone having come to terms with life and death.

Frederik was just beginning to get interested in Sufism, but very little was ever said openly about it by any of the family. In fact, at that time I felt more intrigued by Ali Khan as a person than I was by his philosophy, of which I knew nothing. I always felt slightly confused by the secrecy and low-toned voices behind closed doors.

In late June we returned to work with Kate Rosén on the staging of our act, which was done on the front lawn of Piniehøj with help from Osorio's howling each time Frederik picked up the guitar.

Copenhagen is a very small town when it comes to knowing what everyone else is up to, so within a day or so, the number of friends who announced intentions of coming to that first night would have filled a medium-sized theatre. That's why I'll be forever grateful to Fritz for letting us "sneak open" the night before to get the feel of performing before facing all our friends.

I'd had two dresses made for our engagement, a white and a black, and chose the white one for the preview. We did our three songs in an eternity of terror for me, and once offstage, I burst into tears. This had nothing to do with the total effect, but with my falling down on the technical fine points remembered from my studies with Élé. It took me ages to learn that these were really immaterial to the artistry of the performance. Frederik, who had never studied voice and, hence, had no such problem, consoled me as I wailed, "I don't want to do this! Can't we get out of it?" But, back we went for the premiére of "Nina and Frederik." Being superstitious, I permanently scrapped the white dress.

I knew, or knew of, everyone who was there opening night. I have always hated performing when I know people in the audience and am much happier in a stadium of thirty thousand strangers than in a small club with a few familiar faces scattered about. No one is himself on stage, and I find this highly embarrassing in front of those who knew the real me, but I'm getting used to it—finally. The repertoire we'd assembled since our contract-signing was mostly calypsos and folk songs, backed by a four-piece rhythm group or Frederik's guitar alone. Much to our surprise, we were well received.

A TV show called "Copenhagen at Night" would televise live a different nightspot in the city every Saturday, and a week after opening it was Mon Coeur's turn. The show made us an overnight sensation. Our material was totally different (folk songs at that time—1957—were appreciated only among university students), and so was our style and background. The background worked in both good and bad ways for us over the years, I think. The publicity generated immediately was enormous, but the professional assessment was of two amateurs with no theatrical background—instant success, but it couldn't last. It did, however, but we had to work extra hard and extra long to overcome the stigma of "society kids dabbling in music."

My stepfather was very ill then and, sadly, was never able to see us perform in Mon Coeur, but my mother was there beaming every night, and the whole summer social scene just moved from Piniehøj to Tivoli Gardens.

We were held over another six weeks, then had an offer from Lulu Ziegler, a well-known Danish *chanteuse-diseuse,* to do two months in her literary cabaret in Stockholm. By then, we'd also cut our first record. Bent Fabricius-Bjerre, director of Metronome Records, looked us up one night after the show.

"Would you like to cut a record?"

"Yes."

"When?"

"Monday."

"It's settled."

No contract, just a verbal agreement, a rare thing in show business, but then Bent is a rare person. At this recording session, we met Jørn Grauengaard, who had his own group and who eventually became our teacher, mentor and close friend. But at that first meeting, he really despaired. For openers, we didn't know how many bars there were to a song. That was a problem we'd never considered.

"How do you think we all come out together?" he sarcastically inquired.

But his patience was limitless, we eventually did settle the amount of bars, and the record was a smash success. Before accepting the engagement in Stockholm, we now had to decide whether this "lark" was to become serious business. With talk afoot of our doing a movie, Fritz suggested he become our manager, and we thought we'd give it a try.

It was in Stockholm that I got my first good lesson in show business. Lulu, with all of us assembled one day for rehearsal, turned to me and said, "Now, you've got to forget all your fine society manners and start getting into the nitty-gritty and guts of it all. Stop putting on airs and being so stiff and cold."

Everyone—Frederik, the musicians, the other performers, the stagehands—was there, and I was utterly humiliated, but she was right, of course. (I'd always been raised knowing there were a lot of things people might think but just wouldn't say.) I was grateful for her candor afterward.

Our stay in Stockholm was a success, too. I've listened at times to our earliest recordings and find them not bad at all. There's the happy and joyful innocence of the amateur, and it sort of works, I with my pure, reedy voice and Frederik with his natural sense of the performer.

We were still using our original black costumes from the

125

Tivoli, being superstitious, and they were getting very tatty, but I wouldn't give them up. So I went all the way, tore off the sleeves, ripped the hem and sewed on big patches of bright yellow and orange. We finally shed the shoes and performed barefoot. Our original idea for simple black outfits had been to negate the traditional ideas of nightclub costumes and the ethnic imagery usually associated with folk music. The total effect was not unlike two glamorous scarecrows.

We returned to Copenhagen "in triumph," to use the words that ran through all the newspaper and magazine clippings, causing a national excitement not too different from the Beatles several years later in England. Once, when we sang at the opening of a marathon bicycle race in Denmark, we wore bright red sweaters. Immediately, everything was being painted or manufactured in "Calypso Red"—lipsticks, wall paints, clothing, pots and pans, bicycles, even prams. Red and black became the two colors we used for years to come.

We soon knew the experience of being mobbed by fans. Our hair was pulled, our clothes were ripped and, on one occasion, four persons had to be carted off in ambulances. We received sacks of mail, some funny, most just saying "thank you," a few containing nonsense from the cranks and crabs in the world and a few separate declarations of love, much to our amusement. In some ways I think we were before our time, both in attire and in making folk and ethnic music a commercial success, the first such act in Europe. It was interesting to watch it happen later in America with Peter, Paul and Mary, Bob Dylan and Joan Baez.

Into the midst of our dazzling new-found fame came Hugo Wessel, anxious to find what indeed was going on that I hadn't gotten to the top of the Danish immigration quota list for America. The truth is, I knew the list was very long and, with the excitement of my new career, had just tried to put the inevitable confrontation out of my head. But as long as he was back, ensconced in the guest villa at Piniehøj, I decided I must give our marriage one more try. It was a bit bizarre, one must admit, to go home to Hugo after working with Frederik all day.

126

Just before starting our first film, "The Richest Girl in The World," my stepfather died after a long and courageous battle with cancer. During his illness he had entrusted the running of his business to others, and through mismanagement the firm had suffered great financial losses. The extent of these my mother kept from him and was determined, despite these grave reversals, that he would die in the same house he'd been born in and enjoyed all his life. The devotion and consideration each showed the other during these long and difficult years was a remarkable and beautiful thing to see. Not until his last three days in a coma did her strength suddenly falter, and for the only time in my life did she allow me to be her pillar of support. My sister had come home from a broken marriage, so it was a painful year.

Without my stepfather, my mother felt lonely in the big house. Piniehøj was sold a year after to a land developer who had the tactlessness to say to my mother as she offered to show him her home, "That won't be necessary. We're going to bulldoze it anyway." He did, trees and all, and the site is now occupied by twenty-eight bungalows. I've never driven past there again.

"The Richest Girl in The World" became one of the biggest box-office hits Denmark had ever known. Cleverly conceived so as not to require much acting, it had us on the run all through the picture, and we appeared only now and then, mainly to sing. But, we were *talked* about all the time!

Meanwhile, Fritz was busy arranging tours, one of which took us to Iceland. In spite of its isolation and lack of wealth, its people overwhelmed us with their generosity and hospitality. It's the only place I've found most of the women in each night's audience dressed in their national costumes.

The gulf between Hugo and me had become unbridgeable. The reconciliation attempts had failed and I wanted my freedom. I couldn't face any more arguments with him, nor the ensuing endless family conferences. Quietly putting a suitcase into the back of the car, I wrote a letter to Hugo and left for a ten o'clock "appointment with the dentist." Actually I took a plane to Milan: after all this turmoil, I craved escape in

127

music. For two weeks, I spent every evening at La Scala, and lazy days reading and going to all the museums. My choice had been perfect: no one who knew me knew I was there, and no one there knew me at all. I even saw Maria Callas one afternoon as I was passing the opera. To me she'd always been "La Divina," the greatest of them all, and I just stood there staring. My food intake consisted of working my way through all thirty-four flavors in the ice cream parlor around the corner from my hotel. Finally I called Frederik, and we met in Corsica two days later.

We had drifted into love, having known each other so well for so long. It was not a mad, instant flash that strikes total strangers like a bolt of lightning. We were happy working together and didn't talk of marriage. When he arrived in Ajaccio, we rented a scooter, checked all our gear except for bathing suits, toothbrushes and sweaters, and went off to Corsican points unknown. It was glorious freedom!

We headed north along the rock coast until we hit a dirt road seemingly leading nowhere, followed it for a couple of miles and ended up in front of a small seaside house which turned out to be, in the owner's words, a hotel. The proprietor, a stocky weather-beaten old Corsican with a white brush-cut that bristled more or less according to his moods, rented out his three rooms to French spearfishermen. He himself lived in a cluttered room off the bar with a red-haired over-the-hill Marseilles whore (by her own admission). He ran the kitchen and bar, she handled the rest of the chores. There were no vacancies, so he let us use his aunt's otherwise closed-up house farther across the rocks, where we lived in the only unlocked room: pink walls, tiled floor, two candles, a basin and pitcher, outdoor plumbing and a huge brass bed.

We stayed there a month. The neighboring fishermen would drop us off on the small rocky islands in the mornings to swim and fish and lunch on fresh local goat's cheese, bread and wine, then pick us up in late afternoon. At night, they would join us in a game of poker and gamble for glasses of *cap corse,* the sweet liqueur of the region. During busy evenings, that is the nights the goatherds brought their cheeses, we would all sing and play the guitar.

One night Frederik rummaged through his knapsack and brought out what I can only describe as a mini horse-turd. With a secretive air he told me it was something he'd gotten from Morocco, something called "hash," supposed to have the same effect as a lot of champagne. Never having heard of drugs, and appreciating his reference, I figured it couldn't be all bad. We made it into the most revolting stewlike tea! Drinking the stuff was nauseating, and the only thing I recall was that it made us both very giggly. But then, having had our share of *cap corses* that evening, no wonder.

Sundays, the nearby villagers would descend en masse for lunch al fresco. I waited on tables, did the dishes in the grass and cranked the postman's gramophone (on lone only on Sundays). Frederik and I often enlarged the menu with iodine-tasting sea urchins (the Corsicans loved them), which we'd caught earlier in the day. After all the festivity we would sit in the sun with our "host and hostess" and talk till nightfall. We've never spent a happier time together.

Frederik left a few days before me to go home via Holland. Back in Copenhagen, I found tempers had simmered down and peacefully got a divorce in two weeks. (To me, a failing marriage could not be held together by tradition and the old unwritten laws of society. We were into a totally new era. The young generation in Europe was suddenly independent in self and money, throwing nationalities, class, color and religion overboard and becoming masters of their own lives. We were at the threshold of the '60's, and the whole picture was changing.) I asked only that my paperweight collection and few antiques be sent to me. I never got them. I guess they're still being used by Hugo's wealthy friends in Santa Barbara. Maybe they need them more than I do.

It didn't take long for Frederik and me to snap back into the professional aspects of our lives. Fritz had arranged a heavy schedule of appearances in Denmark and throughout Europe. Hugo left shortly afterward. I've seen him only once since, a sort of "High Noon" scene in Malaga, when only mad dogs and two Danes were out in the midday sun. He was coming from the north, I from the south, and he pretended he didn't see me. At the time, I was en route to my obstetrician, nine months pregnant, clad in one of my Marimekko specials and as unavoidable as a bright yellow two-ton truck. I stopped him and we chatted for a while, but the thing that struck me was that he looked exactly as he had fourteen years before—not a wrinkle, not a line, no change in expression.

Frederik
and Nina

That winter our second movie started. The film, "Melody of Love," had a well-worn plot: boy meets girl, boy loses girl, boy ends up with girl (what else could they do with an established singing couple!) As the filming began, Louis Armstrong arrived in Copenhagen to do some concerts, and he was written into the last scenes before the rest of the script had even been completed. We visited him often during his stay. In his warm-hearted generous way he had the extraordinary quality of making you feel the focus of his full attention even in a crowded room, and everyone simultaneously felt the same thing. Lucille, his wife, was beautiful. Through the years, we'd send messages of hello whenever mutual friends would be heading their way.

Ole Schmidt, the well-known Danish composer and conductor at the Royal Theatre, was to score the film. Often after working late, we'd all go back to Frederik's flat and have sent up from the local restaurant luke-warm duck, two dozen oysters, aquavit, Chateauneuf du Pape and whatever else sounded good at the moment. After all this gourmet inspiration, very ostentatious and quite beyond our means (but then, "Hell! We're making a *movie!*"), Ole would begin banging away at the piano, and the next door neighbor would being banging

131

away at Frederik's door, it being 3:00 A.M. more likely than not. Ole's standard rejoinder was:

"Do you live here?"

"Yes . . ."

"And do you pay the rent here?"

"Well, yes . . ."

"Well then, go back to bed!" Ole's logic was that the rent on the flat was so enormous that if anyone lived within those overpriced walls, he could damned well do as he pleased.

On the last day of shooting, I was the only one of us three who had to report for work. Ole had an enormous appetite for good food and drink, and he and Frederik decided we were all going to a country inn for lunch, *"Basta!"* They conned me into calling the studio pretending to be ill, and we took off in Frederik's new Volvo. Heading down Highway #1, Frederik was at the wheel, Ole next to him and I stretched across the back seat asleep. Suddenly, a huge sand truck veered across the highway just ahead of us. When its driver saw that we were unable to stop, he jammed on his brakes rather than hitting the accelerator. We smashed full speed into the truck, the Volvo's steel frame the only thing that kept us from going completely under it. Ole was nearly scalped, Frederik somehow escaped with only minor cuts and I was knocked unconscious.

My first recollection was waking up in the ditch with an ambulance driver speaking to me—I never found out his name to thank him for his kindnesses—with only black-and-white vision, just like early TV, a numb wet face and a splitting headache. The vision problem bothered me for the first few moments of consciousness, but then real panic set in: what would Preben Phillipsen, the producer, say when he learned we'd played hooky from the set? I'd never missed work ever, so the guilt was compounded by the instant "justice" I'd just experienced. All of us were carted off to the nearest hospital to be stitched and examined and observed, during which time my color vision returned. Ole was the most seriously injured. I remember his lying unconscious on a stretcher in the hallway, his head a mess of blood, and suddenly sitting bolt upright to comment: "Well, as long as we're not bored!" then

132

passing out again. Ever since, I've often thought of that line in good times, and in bad.

Besides the producer's imagined wrath, I also feared they'd have to shave my hair to patch up my head, which had been cut on top. I kept after Frederik to make sure they didn't, but the clear plastic spray bandage made things just as bad as it didn't wash out. I finished the movie in a hat, and Ole, thank God, recovered completely. Just a plug for one aspect of socialized medicine: this six-day hospital jaunt cost me only one dollar.

The rest of '59 saw our career and travel horizons expanding rapidly. One day we were in the midst of doing a TV show when Preben Phillipsen called.

"How would you like to go to Russia the day after tomorrow?"

Although not actually competing, he was showing "Melody of Love" at the Moscow Film Festival, a great excuse for going.

We flew from Copenhagen to Moscow in a Russian plane, an airborne replica of a 1920's railroad car right down to the red plush. Surrendering our passports at Moscow Airport was an uncomfortable feeling, though apparently part of the procedure. Frederik had been there in Stalin's era and assured us things had eased considerably. However, an intensive search for bugging devices in our rooms was still our first order of business, producing no results, much to our disappointment. We were assigned an interpreter who spoke remarkably good English. As a matter of fact, all the interpreters spoke impeccable French or English, yet none had ever been out of the Soviet Union. It was extraordinary and a bit scary.

With our special film festival badges, we visited the Kremlin and all the usual sights but bypassed all the mile-long queues. In those days, both Lenin and Stalin were on view. Lenin looked a bit under the weather and, if I remember correctly, they closed the tomb shortly after to glue on his ear. Having brought some of my more glamorous clothes and stiletto heels, I caused a sensation. At that point, there hadn't been many western tourists in Moscow, and in G.U.M., the huge

133

department store, women would come up to touch the material of my dress. They'd jabber away in Russian, I'd babble back in English, and we'd all smile, laugh and embrace. I found the Russians warm and outgoing, and gifts were lavished upon me by total strangers all through our stay.

We took the very impressive Underground and visited the permanent fair of all the Soviet states, where I was intrigued by the 360-degree movie. It required the audience to sit in the middle, a bit uncommercial in its limitations, I should imagine, but fascinating nonetheless. Our guide was a schoolteacher, a lovable girl with endless patience and obvious pride in her country. She was on call 'round the clock and had a ready (if rehearsed) answer for everything, the most common being, "You can get it, but it isn't practical" whenever I asked about something I didn't see around.

We all went to the "Tivoli Gardens" of Moscow to see the puppet theatre and a special performance given by eight members of the Leningrad Ballet. I was moved to tears by the prima ballerina's interpretation of a melting icicle, but jolted back to reality by Preben's dry Danish voice next to me saying, "That reminds me of an ice cube in a glass of whisky."

We ended six marvelous days by appearing on Russian television: although we'd said we wouldn't sing, in the midst of the live interview, Frederik's guitar was brought onstage and we had no choice (the guitar had been fetched from the hotel by the TV staff during the show).

Back in Scandinavia, there were constant articles about "The Beautiful Couple," the embarrassing name we got stuck with, always with subtle inquiries about when, if ever, we would marry. My mother was more tactful than the press in this matter and only occasionally wondered when I'd get out of this overextended lark and settle down. Frankly, we were in doubt as to how long our career would last and several times had talked of quitting after one of our really bad squabbles. During one of those, I was the cause of Frederik's losing his temper and his guitar. Whenever we recorded, the first few takes would usually be the best. Some artists pick a performance to pieces in search of perfection, but with us such repetition drove out the spontaneity and the performance grew stale. The simplest songs were always the most difficult: I'll never know why. One day we were recording a little folk song with just the guitar and were into the eleventh take when again I opened my big mouth. Frederik, already impatient and angry, exploded. The guitar flew straight across the room at me, but I ducked. It crashed into the grand piano and was no more. and the grand piano didn't look too good, either. This was all recorded for posterity and for many laughs later—but it wasn't funny then. Both of us were hesitant about marriage, I for obvious reasons, Frederik feeling too young to cope with the responsibilities of wife and family.

Once again we packed our suitcases. The closest I'd come to experiencing Venice was singing "The Tales of Hoffman"; now I was off on location there doing a German picture, "Mandolinen und Mondschein." It was a technicolor extravaganza of germanically romanticized bourgeois life and rather dreadful, but I spent two weeks in a gondola doing long shots, so I had no reason to complain. Frederik and I waltzed in full moonlight on St. Mark's Square, accompanied by Fritz Rutzika and his yapping dogs. Fritz was one of the most lovable nuts I've known—I've laughed with him more than anyone except Frederik. He had such middle-European charm coupled with a heavy accent, he could get away with murder. Among his luggage were always two life-size papier-mâché bulldogs. He loved to set them down in a café, activate their very realistic barking and startle the heavily laden unsuspecting waiters. And, he didn't limit their yapping only to cafés—they carried on in airports, hotel lobbies, everywhere—while we pretended not to know him. Although he'd spent several years in Auschwitz, he still liked working in Germany and felt on home ground in Berlin where we did the last six weeks of the picture.

He had the habit of rolling up his shirt sleeve to show off his Auschwitz tattoo number. I never quite figured out why he did it, except for possibly savoring the shocked reaction he always got.

We had to speak German in the picture. Having had little

135

practice, it was a real struggle in the beginning, but we got unexpected help from our fellow actors and crew. From the first day, no one except the producer spoke or understood English—until the last day at the cast party. Suddenly, almost everybody knew a passable amount. I still sweat to think of what Frederik and I (we speak English to each other) might have said to each other thinking no one would understand.

With Jørn Grauengaard and his group, we did a tour of Swedish folk parks in August. These were oftimes merely a stage set up in the woods, surrounded by a few amusements like carousels, shooting tents and such, and lit more by the all-night glow of Swedish summer skies than by electricity. People came from miles around. One night while singing to an audience of more than five thousand, it suddenly started to rain. As if by signal, nearly five thousand umbrellas of every possible color sprang open, the instant blooming of a gigantic bed of flowers. En route we ran into an elk who'd dashed into our path on a dark road. The front of the car was smashed beyond repair, and the elk had to be shot by a game warden. I can still see the eyes of the animal as it lay there, wounded and helpless.

Another vacation saw Frederik off to visit friends and family while I holidayed in Sardinia with my cousin Klaus. His mother had died in childbirth, and he'd spent a lot of time with us during his father's assignments for the Danish Intelligence Service. For years, when I was very small, I used to faithfully put a sugar lump for the stork on Mother's window still, hoping for an older brother. Klaus became the next best thing and, looking alike, we often were taken for brother and sister.

We drove from Geneva in my brand new Karmann Ghia convertible (Klaus's father never forgave me for buying a German car), and took the boat from Civitaveccia to Sardinia. There we stayed in a small fishing village next to Arbatax for two dollars a day, meals included, and the only other guests were a German couple.

There was lots of snorkeling by day and frequent trips at dusk to the village for coffee and wine in the few cafés. On these excursions, we often saw skulking about in the alleys the shadowy figure of a man secretively hunched over, hiding something. Once he looked up, was caught in a shaft of light, and I saw that half his face was so hideously distorted that the features were completely out of place. Six years later, I recognized the face in a pictorial weekly. A Swedish brain surgeon had gone to the same village on holiday, met the poor man and brought him back to Stockholm. There, the surgeon operated, discovered a tremendous cyst, removed it and successfully remodeled the man's entire facial structure. Whenever I think of Sardinia, I always remember that miraculous story.

Toward the end of our three weeks, we were running short of funds and, to make matters worse, Klaus had all of his money stolen out of the car. We had just enough for the balance of our bill, and for coffee and petrol to get us to Hamburg, where I had an engagement. After loading the car on to the ferry, Klaus set off to have a talk with the crew—no way was I going to sleep in the car, he said. Ten minutes later, I was solemnly ushered down to the fourteen-bunk crew's cabin and presented with a freshly made-up berth. All the pin-ups on the walls had been carefully covered and the place obviously cleaned in a great hurry. There I spent the night all by myself. Lord knows where the crew slept, but the next morning we drank a wine toast in thanks and farewell, and took off on our nonstop eighty-two-hour drive to Hamburg.

To go into each one of Frederik's and my engagements during the next winter would be impossible. Came spring, 1960, nerves were frayed, tempers were flaring and we again had quit the business and each other at least a dozen times. Splitting up for a while was to be the test. We drove to Geneva together, then parted company, I heading for Rome, he for Spain.

Since I had no time schedule, I explored the backroad areas of Italy, driving all through the Apennines, stopping off to see what was doing in Florence and staying at whatever inns appealed to me. Late one afternoon the car stalled. I ran out of gas—one of my favorite gambles, which I often lose—not too far from Orvieto, a beautiful town perched high on a giant rock formation in the mountains of Tuscany. There wasn't a soul in sight and it was growing dark, so I locked up the car and walked to the nearest house. The place, as it turned out, was a small country bar with a few tables, a TV set and the same Coca-Cola posters found all over the world. The people spoke only Italian; I spoke none. While I was desperately trying to explain my problem in a mixture of French and Spanish with an Italian lilt, three sharply dressed men drove up. From what I could gather, they were telling the others that they would take care of me. The first group became very excited. They took me aside and made it quite clear—despite the language barrier—that if I went with the three men, they would surely rob and rape me once they got me alone. Such incidents happened all the time, they said! The whole thing became a huge shouting match, and finally someone got on the phone to the police. Apparently, it was considered very dangerous for unescorted ladies like me to be driving alone through the countryside, especially at night, so my "hosts" were protecting me. They arranged a police escort for the hour's drive to Orvieto and, to be absolutely safe, installed the local shepherd in the front seat next to me to "ride shotgun." Not only did they fill up the gas tank, but they refused payment for it. While we were waiting for the police convoy to arrive, I was royally waited upon in the bar. All kinds of food and wine were brought out—again, no payment—and the peasants came streaming in from all over to discuss and cluck over the near-disaster I'd been plucked from. It's the sort of thing that happens to me time and time again—very reassuring for one's faith in humanity.

Once in Rome, I found a moderate, nondescript hotel and set out on foot to get to know the city. On one of my first strolls, I heard a voice in Danish calling out my name. It was a very pretty girl, Nini, with green eyes and long hair. She was enrolled in the film school and lived in a tiny *pensione* on the Plaza Fontana de Trevi. It had a vacancy, so I moved in. Marked only by a door in the wall, it was very cheap and very basic, but what a view! An elderly gentleman who never seemed to get out of his pajamas used to sit by the front door and screen everyone who walked in or out. He'd lock the door altogether at midnight, and getting him out of bed after that hour was a real problem. I attended the film school with Nini for a while but I missed Frederik. Three months of being carefree and single (and Rome wasn't a bad place for that at all) was enough, and I made ready to leave.

Meanwhile, Frederik was getting around in his own way, commuting between Marbella and Seville. Whereas I was playing the field, he'd gotten caught, so when I finally turned up in Marbella, I was a far from welcome sight. She was a very wealthy eighteen-year-old German, with endless credit cards, furs, jewels, Ferrari and chauffeur. She'd never met anything quite like Frederik and doted upon every word he uttered. I can't say I blame her—nor him, for she was lovely. That threw a spoke into my wheels. I went home to Copenhagen and nervously chewed my fingernails, waiting—and hoping—for him to get fed up with it all. Eventually, Marbella and its whole scene must have lost its novelty, for one day I received a simple wire: "Will you take back an old friend? Frederik."

He came directly to Copenhagen, we then went to London for a singing date and finally announced our engagement to stop all the speculations. One thing we didn't want was a lot of publicity around the wedding, so we decided to get married very quickly in Puplinge near Geneva, where I had often stayed with Frederik's family the last two years. The village had no more than twelve or fourteen houses in those days, and the local street cleaner was also the mayor. The only guests were my mother, my sister and her new husband, Frederik's parents, his sister and brother-in-law and eight close friends we were able to round up with no advance notice.

My future parents-in-law, upon retirement, had moved to Geneva where they'd bought and renovated a farmhouse in Puplinge near the French border. It was not large but very warm and cozy, full of their favorite things inherited and accumulated in travels throughout the world.

September 21, 1960 was a warm, cloudy day, but the house was so filled with flowers, it seemed more like spring than the

139

first day of autumn. At noontime family and guests marched from the house down the road to the schoolhouse, which also doubled as offices for the mayor/street cleaner. Just before leaving I discovered some journalists and photographers lurking in the garden and became so furious at this intrusion that I refused to take one step out the door. After a while I calmed down, and we eventually began the procession. The mayor was in his upstairs office in his Sunday best, brooms discreetly tucked away. But I suddenly saw a male figure in the shadows near the door. Thinking him to be yet another journalist, I slammed the door in his face and barricaded it. To my slightly myopic embarrassment, I found he was really the schoolteacher who was only delivering our wedding rings. (After the ceremony, I was so swept up by the emotion of it all that I once again took him for someone he wasn't—my new brother-in-law—and threw my arms about him, kissing and hugging him. Ever after he was never quite comfortable when meeting me on the street!)

The ceremony was short and simple, and the only special decoration was the potbellied stove covered in white flowers all the way up the pipe. Once the schoolteacher had recovered from door-slammings and bear hugs, he took us downstairs and introduced us to the children. They lined up and sang for us, then eagerly dug into the petits fours ordered for the occasion.

We trooped back to the house for champagne and *kransekage* (the traditional conical-shaped Danish wedding cake). In one breath, I had become the wife of Frederik Jan Gustav Floris van Pallandt, and a Dutch citizen. It was one of the happiest moments of my life, and I was so optimistic and confident of the future. Nothing could mar my joy, not even Frederik's little speech to me about his having to keep in contact with his German girl friend for a special sort of "soul relationship" that she apparently fulfilled and I did not. Love and patience, I told myself—and turned back to the champagne. As it turned out, the "soul communication" only lasted a few months.

The wedding luncheon was held at Geneva's elegant old

Des Eaux Vives, right on the lake. The menu was a gourmet's delight, but by that time we'd all been on a three-day prenuptial culinary spree, so the speeches drew more attention than the food. In keeping with Danish custom, these were many and funny. My mother spoke, too, of course—in fact, she made all of four speeches, for every time she was halfway through, she'd burst into tears and have to sit down to pull herself together and start again. In the evening, the younger group went to a play in Spanish in the Civic Theatre. What prompted us to do that, I'll never know, for the only one who spoke Spanish properly was Frederik. One of the wedding guests, Michael Meyer, a playwright from London and a great wit, gave an hilarious running commentary and translation of the play for the rest of us, and we so misbehaved we were asked to leave after the second act.

Our bridal suite that night was a downstairs room at the farmhouse into which Frederik's grandfather's fourposter had been moved. The bed, which had been made in the Virgin Islands where his grandfather had been governor, was only six feet long, a fact that no one had taken into consideration. Frederik is six-foot-four.

When we descended the stairs that evening, having bid everyone a goodnight, we opened the door and discovered the mothers had been at work. There were flowers all over the room, my wedding bouquet was carefully placed at the foot of the bed, and upon the bed itself were new monogrammed sheets and my best nightgown carefully arranged and pinched in at the waist. A bottle of champagne and two glasses were on ice, a glass of water on either bedside night table—to us, it had the very definite air of a medieval royal bedding down! With all that planning and splendor, we didn't have the heart to tell anyone that, because of the bed's dimensions, I had slept on the floor!

The next morning we packed up and drove off to Germany to do a television show, and that was our honeymoon. Word by this time had gotten out to the press, and for weeks after the media had a field day with the wedding and marriage of —there it was again—"The Beautiful Couple." What really

141

amused us were the pairs of animals—hippos in the Copenhagen zoo, snow leopards in London, even ordinary house pets —being named after us. Several years later when I was late in having our second child, my mother was in Copenhagen listening to the news. The announcer reported: "It's a girl for Frederik and Nina . . ." Well, she thought, it's about time. " . . . and," continued the report, "mother and the sixteen-pound baby are doing fine." It was the hippos.

In December, we had a three-week engagement at the Savoy in London and, by that time, I was pregnant and permanently morning-sick. There was nothing I felt less like doing than getting all dolled up every night and singing. I'd throw up, repair my eye makeup, rush on stage, do my forty-five minutes and rush off to be sick all over again. In those days we couldn't tell anyone, for it wasn't yet fashionable to be pregnant on stage. Of course the smell of food as we did the show didn't help—it was the longest three-week stint I've ever endured. I spent most of my time in bed, making few attempts at sight-seeing. Passing a fish-and-chips stand would send me dashing straight home. One of the few bright moments was when Leonard Cohen, an old friend of Frederik's from Montreal, would come and sit by my bedside to talk while I gorged myself on oranges.

I'd never been so glad to see snow and Geneva as I was when we returned for Christmas.

On Christmas Eve, Frank Powis appeared on our doorstep. He was another old friend of Frederik's from Canada and I'd often heard wild stories of some of their escapades, but had never met him till that night.

Frank stayed with us on and off for the next nine years, became our sometime road manager, "lightning rod," moving man, father confessor and very close and dear friend. He was quite a lad with the ladies, but to this day nobody has been able to pin him down. While first in Geneva with us, he was seeing two girls at one time. One he'd had us invite to stay at the house. (Now, I've always been used to house guests and love to entertain, but I can't stand the type of guest I categorize as a "bathroom messer." That's the type who leaves wet

142

towels in a heap on the floor, wads of hair in the sink, and junk strewn all over the place—that's the type this girl was.) Frank, after a few days with her, was suddenly called off "on business" to Annemasse just across the French border.

While he was with his other girl friend, we were left coping with the first half of his "Captain's Paradise." One day I had had enough and rang him up. "Frank, get this slag out of here!" I said in my most controlled voice. He concluded his "business" in Annemasse in a hurry and was home that afternoon to put the girl on the evening train.

Frederik, Frank and I spent many evenings that spring playing hearts, blackjack and backgammon. Frederik is not a very good loser, so Frank and I deliberately cheated, using blatant foot signals and other devices. We gleefully watched and waited till Frederik would finally throw his cards into my vast sea of orange peels and furiously stalk out of the room. Thinking about it now, it was a dirty trick, but we were all so good-humored, it really didn't matter. Also, it didn't take him long to figure things out, for I never could keep a straight face.

Our parents-in-law had left for Marbella, in part to let us be on our own, so the three of us spent five months "hatching" in total bliss. Frederik brought home a new car, a Morgan. That's one of those contraptions that only the English, with their predilection for physical discomfort, could invent. It was so hard-sprung that a pebble on the road would send your kidneys flying. The wind would howl and blow through the car even with the windows closed, and the soft top leaked. To top it all with my enormous stomach I couldn't even get behind the steering wheel. I had one ride in it, and as it bounced down the road like a stiff-legged frog, Frederik, who liked his comfort, too, had to admit it wasn't quite his cup of tea. It may have been his last fling before fatherhood, but he wasn't that unhappy the day he turned it in.

During this period, I had a great deal of time to read and became particularly fascinated with books on jungle expeditions, like *The Rivers Run East.* There were horrific descriptions of snakes, anacondas in particular. I have always been deathly afraid of snakes, but I couldn't put the book down

143

even then. Just as I'd be completely bug-eyed, fully expecting a hungry reptile to slither right out of the pages, Frederik and Frank would steal up behind my chair and go *"sssssssssssss!"* I'd scream and leap into the air (as much as I could leap), and they, of course, thought it *very* funny. From then on, I always picked my "snake days" when they were out of the house. Since we were temporarily out of work, Frederik busied himself co-authoring a Danish movie script with its director and writing its theme song. He also put some money into it, a not so successful aspect of the venture, but still it was good for him to work on his own.

One June evening, after spending the afternoon sitting in a cherry tree eating half its fruit, I was fixing dinner for the three of us when I suddenly felt awful. Just retribution for my gluttony, no doubt, but the pain persisted. At dinner I picked at my plate, and finally decided it was time to organize the trip to the maternity clinic in Geneva. En route, though, we found time for coffee and cream cakes, much to the chagrin of my stern Swiss doctor.

At Bois-Gentil clinic, I was put to bed in my own room where Frederik and Frank immediately set up the backgammon board and brought out a bottle of wine. This caused great consternation among the nurses and, when the somewhat premature cigars came out, it was instant eviction.

I was left alone feeling sorry for myself all that night and on into the next morning. Though I'd gone to natural childbirth classes, the doctor finally had to put me under, and with forceps delivery, Nicolas was born at noon. The reason for the difficulty and delay was quite apparent: Nicolas weighted in at *ten* pounds. He mostly resembled a fat boiled shrimp with blue-white hair, but he was the most beautiful thing I had ever seen.

I think the feeling of pure love that sweeps over you when holding your firstborn is the closest you'll ever come to godliness in this life. It was June 10, 1961, and Nicolas was a Gemini.

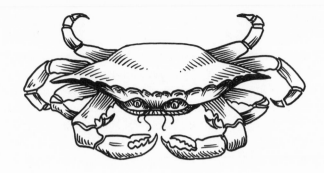

When he was three weeks old, we moved into
our first home, a thatched-roof stone and beam
cottage we'd bought that spring in Høsterkøb, about halfway
between Copenhagen and Elsinore. Frederik and I had looked
for such a place while he was working on the movie script in
Copenhagen and when a theatrical producer friend of ours
decided to sell this place, he gave us first crack at it.

Located on a crayfish-filled inland pond, it had a big vegetable garden, lawns and large rosebeds, an entire nursery and
dozens of fruit trees. It was straight out of Hans Christian
Andersen—too good to be true. But, warned a local cleric at
the time of our purchase, the people in this small, somewhat
inbred farming community were quite strange. In no time at
all, we found that to be absolutely true.

Frederik went on three weeks ahead of me and Nicolas to
fix things up. I'd already picked out everything—curtains,
rugs, paint, wallpaper and colors, and my mother and his
parents had given us whatever we needed to supplement our
wedding gifts. Both families had moved from larger to smaller
homes, so their largesse was not just pots and pans, but furni-

ture, paintings and the lovely things one likes to keep in the family.

Because of the insatiable curiosity of the press, we decided to have an open house for them. That way, we figured, we'd get the whole thing over in a couple of days and no one of the Fourth Estate would feel slighted. The press were great—they got their stories, played with the baby, took their pictures and then left us alone. Our neighbors presented a radically different situation.

Once the news had gotten out that we'd bought the house, even before we'd moved in and were still painting, curious people started picnicking on our lawns and walking in the gardens, hoping to see God knows what. After we'd moved in, we abided by a longtime custom of allowing some of the peasants the use of a "right-of-way" through our courtyard to the state woods behind. The rest of the locals seized upon this as open access to our property, reclassifying it in their minds as the new amusement park.

Our next door neighbor was no help whatsoever—in fact, he was one of the worst. A day or so after we'd moved in, we went over with a bottle of sherry to pay a courtesy call and be good-neighborly. He accepted the sherry, but a few mornings later we found he had dumped all his garbage into our garden. I've never yet figured out the reasons for his actions. Nearly every day he would stand on the main road directing traffic to our house, like a sightseeing shill. We often had up to ten cars in the driveway. When there was no more room there, people would park across the lake and haul out high-powered binoculars, to make up for the disappointment of not being able to smell what I was cooking for dinner. It was horrible. Another neighbor's reaction to us was no less hostile. When we rang *his* doorbell with a bottle of sherry and introduced ourselves, his reply was: "You think you're somebody because you're famous and have a title, but we're going to show you otherwise!" and he banged the door in our faces.

The day of Nicolas's christening in the local church, the old miserable neighbor did his best to chase our guests away by running after them waving his walking stick. One he nearly

146

caught happened to be Princess Viggo, my godmother, but she defended herself successfully by shaking her silver fox in his face.

Eight o'clock one Sunday morning, I came downstairs without a stitch on to fetch Nicolas's bottle and found a family of six, grandfather and all, peering through the window at me. Completely forgetting in my fury that I was stark naked, I ran to the door and, if it hadn't been so well latched, would probably have chased them right through the garden onto the main road.

We decided to build a stockade fence across the driveway, leaving the gate unlatched for those who needed to get through. It looked like something from a Western. The same night it was completed, we heard a big crunching noise. All the locals had banded together and backed a large truck into our fence, trying to tear it down. It was obviously impossible to ask these people nicely to help us keep our home private. Frederik's temper during those summer months had been put to the test and had often flared uncontrollably. Just before we gave up, the neighbor decided to harass us by banging on the door all day long. Frederik went beserk, running after him and threatening to kill him. Although he never did lay a hand on him, the police arrived at seven the next morning with a complaint of assault! That did it. It was so horrible and incomprehensible that we put the house—our "dream" house—up for sale after seven weeks of ownership and moved back to Puplinge.

Actually, Nanny and the baby went on ahead to Switzerland, while Frederik and I went straight to England to begin a tour. We were headlining the bill, as we would for several tours in years following, and I think we really saw the tail end of the great variety era. In those days, it was a mixed pleasure to travel in England. The theatres were rarely heated, very drafty and always damp, and the dressing rooms were usually the same and always filthy. Hard to believe, but I got out the hated long knickers from school days and was most unglamourously dressed under my velvet dresses. Often the backdrops seemed leftover from Victorian times, the large

147

spots of humidity on them looking as though a giant dog had been at work. To try to add a bit of glamour and liven up the stage, we'd rent a couple of potted plants from the local nursery. Instead, being mainly palms and hydrangea, they cast a decidedly funereal air on the whole thing. Once I was nearly overcome by a leaking gas lamp, experiencing the feeling of drunken euphoria. A doctor was called who pumped me full of Lord-knows-what and I somehow reeled onto the stage and survived the evening, although I couldn't remember one second of it. I missed Nicolas terribly, and if it hadn't been for my mother-in-law's almost daily letters about every insignificant little burp and smile, I would've packed my suitcases and run home.

However, the warmth of the audiences and the camaraderie and laughs among all the acts on the bill far outweighed the discomforts one had to put up with. This tour had been arranged by two English impresarios, one of whom, John Coast, Frederik and I worked with till the end of our career together.

In late November, we were on the homeward trail but had one more commitment to fulfill before Christmas. With all our household still in transit to Geneva, we learned that we'd been booked to do "The Ed Sullivan Show" in New York. It was quite a mad dash—we flew over on a Friday evening, did the show live that Sunday and returned late Monday. For some reason, the Sullivan talent coordinators thought that "Nina and Frederik" were an adagio team. When they learned we *sang,* they asked that we prove it at an audition at eleven o'clock the next morning. Now, I just cannot sing before sundown, let alone with eight *real* dancers doing bar exercises to an out-of-tune piano at the end of the room. We were set upon two barstools encircled by five or six very efficient-looking gentlemen with yellow pads and pencils poised. Scared as I was, the whole situation was so grotesque that I could only laugh. We sang and they chose two songs, giving no indication whatsoever as to their opinions of us. At rehearsal just before the show, there was no one in sight except Ed Sullivan, watching us from a corner. When we'd finished, he applauded and graciously came to greet us. As if on signal, everyone appeared to echo his approval. Obviously, no one had wanted to take the blame if we'd fallen flat on our faces.

That was our debut in the States, but it was also the only appearance Frederik and I ever made there together. There were many reasons why we didn't pursue a career in the U.S. even though we, like all European performers, knew that making it in America would be the high point of our professional lives. There were family responsibilities, young children we were away from too much already, and more than enough long-range professional commitments elsewhere in the world where we were already established. And, quite frankly, Frederik just didn't want to join the rat race. He had many other things he wanted to do and to be tied down to a two-year U.S. contract, which we had been offered, was unthinkable.

The spring of 1962, we did more TV shows and concerts in Europe and then moved—Frederik, Nicolas (then a year old), the nanny, Frank and I—to Blackpool for the longest running engagement of our career: 180 days. We'd deliberately taken it just to stay in one place for a while and to be able to have Nicolas with us. Again we headed the bill of a large old-fashioned variety show, performing six nights a week and then, on our own, doing one-nighters on Sunday. It was rough, for we were working seven nights a week for nearly six months, but it was a good school for learning one's craft.

Blackpool is unique, an Irish Sea resort not unlike Brighton, but where it seems to rain at least 360 days of the year. The other five, the sunshine so befuddles everyone that the citizenry's main activity is blinking about in a semi-stupor looking for last year's sunglasses. And, although the city is right on the sea, for some mysterious reason all the boardwalk benches face the trolley tracks instead of the water.

The house we rented is best described as a mausoleum or perhaps a memorial to how long the human race can survive without brooms, brushes, soap and water. Carpeting, its color a "most unfortunate brown," covered the floors, and its fluff and lint covered everything else. All the dustings had merely shifted this fluff from one corner to another. The nanny and

I straight away went at it with elbow grease and cartons of Vim, and after three solid weeks of scrubbing found to our amazement that the kitchen floor was really blue and white checkered.

One night soon after we'd arrived, we were sitting around with our musicians when someone thought he saw a rat ambling across the baby grand piano and off behind one of the drapes. I wasn't sure whether it was a joke or not, but when I found rat droppings the next morning, I S.O.S.'ed the Blackpool rat catcher. He was a most delightful man who, when he wasn't spreading rat poison, pursued his hobby of collecting butterflies just as energetically. He came every week to rip up the floorboards to put down more poison and to look for carcasses which, oddly enough, he never found. I was most concerned about the smell if one of our unwelcome guests ate the poison, then crawled off to some inaccessible spot to turn his toes. Fortunately, we never had that problem.

Far exceeding the rats and fluff in fascination was the washing machine. The first time I started it, it did a perfect foxtrot straight across the kitchen floor. By the time I caught it, stopped it and got the thing back to where it belonged, I realized the only way to keep it from dancing right out the door was to sit on it. So every Sunday morning for two hours, I'd sit on it with my Sunday papers and bounce my way from front page to back—even the classifieds and the shipping notices. Who said show business wasn't glamorous!

Our Blackpool show was a collection of vaudeville acts— adagio dancers, jugglers, acrobats—and a wonderful English comedian, Tommy Cooper, whose twice-nightly performance we all watched faithfully. The adagio couple's dressing room was separated from ours by a paper-thin wall. Lovely as they were otherwise, every night after they came off stage, they'd have violent arguments and Frederik and I would instinctively duck as things started flying, sounding as though they'd come sailing right through the wall. It always made me feel slightly embarrassed as though I were eavesdropping.

The show's finale was a true extravaganza. Billed as a Scottish medley, it featured the boys' and girls' choruses, eight

150

bagpipes who always, *always,* tuned up right outside our dressing room, the entire cast and a giant waterfall. The latter had been trucked in by some company who held the theatrical waterfall monopoly for all of Great Britain. It was basically a painted tarpaulin that unfolded in minutes. Then tons of water —real water—cascaded down the tarp, and everyone in the audience gasped in delight. On stage we soon were gasping, too—for fresh air. The *same* water was used every night for five months, and the odor (which luckily never crossed the footlights) was revolting. Speaking of old water, one afternoon Frederik and Frank were in the dining room writing their thirty-eight-act, cast-of-thousands musical version of *Don Quixote.* They'd just taken a break and walked into the kitchen to ask me to make them some tea when the whole dining room ceiling collapsed, completely burying and badly damaging the table at which they'd been working. Apparently, water from a cracked pipe upstairs had been collecting for two months in the space between the ceiling and the second floor, and the whole thing had just let go. The "cast-of-thousands" was washed away, but thankfully Frederik and Frank had escaped.

Blackpool was a lot of fun, but I could see Frederik's restlessness grow day by day. To be stuck in the same place for so long was not his style, and if it hadn't been for the distraction of *Don Quixote,* God knows how he would have lasted.

Back in Geneva with Nicolas, Nanny, Frank and the two of us, I felt quarters were getting both physically and emotionally cramped. I had great respect for my parents-in-law, but I guess I was slightly intimidated, too. It was the old parental authority, even though they'd opened their home to us generously and lovingly. Two generations and four strong wills were contained within four thin walls, and it took a lot of musicality to keep it all in tune. When not working, Frederik spent most of his time with his father, an extremely knowledgeable, intelligent man, and with Frank. Being together twenty-four hours a day during work, with all the attendant stress and tension, plus the added nettle of my being a breadwinner, too, made it especially important for him to have some independent private life. And yet, as much as I understood and encouraged

151

him in this, I was saddened that we never really shared our free time together anymore.

I so much wanted a home of our own, although I rarely dared mention that desire, and then only to Frederik. But it was always put off. Life had become strangely isolated. I suddenly realized we were together all right, but never *alone* together. Our talks had imperceptibly grown into family conferences. His flights of thought were becoming more and more abstract, while mine had been grounded by practicalities. Intuitively, I recognized all of this, yet intellectually I wasn't perceptive enough to reason it out.

There were a few more television shows, and then the Christmas holidays were upon us. Much in need of a vacation, Frederik and I had blocked off a two-month period in our spring schedule for an escape—to Greece, hopefully to buy some land. But with the tags still hanging from a special new wardrobe, I learned to my dismay that I was pregnant again. With delivery scheduled for July, we packed away the Greek travel folders and the new wardrobe, and moved to Marbella to wait for the baby. Originally, the plan was that we were to build a smaller house on my parents'-in-law property there, but at this point, they'd not even finished their own house. With my father-in-law's increasing ill health and the frustrations and problems of building, they gave up the project, asked us to complete it and then put it on the market.

Frank left for his usual retreat on Ibiza. I'd listened night after night to his tales of this magical Spanish island in the Mediterranean with its colony of artistic eccentrics, and had an insatiable curiosity about the place. Frederik was going to Morocco with a writer friend, but as a consolation prize, reluctantly promised he'd first take me to Ibiza for two or three days. After two months of pouring rain in Marbella, we landed in Ibiza in a blaze of sun. In the taxi between the airport and the town of Ibiza, Frederik suddenly turned to me and said, "We don't have to go to Greece. This is where we're going to find a piece of land."

Ibiza that May of '63 was very different from what it is today. There was one small two-prop plane a week from Bar-

152

celona, and the airport consisted of nothing more than a grassy strip and a shed with a corrugated tin roof. Even the windsock had a hole in the heel! There were a few taxis, even fewer private cars, and only two or three paved roads, the rest being the red clay so typical of the island. We installed ourselves in one of the few modern hotels and set out almost immediately to explore.

The first things one notices are the color of the soil, which changes from bright orange to dark bluish-purple, and the architecture, a mixture of Spanish and Moorish style white-washed houses with perfectly proportioned flat-tiled roofs and very small windows. The hills are mainly covered with scrub and pines, the valleys lush with orchards of fruit trees and vegetables and wheat. The droughts over the last ten or fifteen years have seriously marked the island. The mode of irrigation at that time was the same ox-driven water wheel system the Moors had introduced during the mid-1400's. There was hardly any electricity, very few phones and only local produce was available. It was as if Ibiza had lain dormant for centuries and, sadly, we foreigners were the first to awaken her to the twentieth century.

We were very conscious of the complete quiet—no cars, no machinery, only the sounds of nature. Horses and ox carts were all one met on the roads, and one felt like an intruder driving a car past peasant women working in the fields still wearing long billowy skirts, shawls, braids and straw hats. The whole rhythm of life was so different, so attuned to the seasons and in harmony with nature. Life was hard for the peasants, with no modern tools. But, reminiscing years later with my neighboring farmers, I felt that despite the prosperity that tourism has brought, they regret the change in many ways.

In the next three days, we covered most of the island searching for property to buy. I wanted to be right on the sea, but Frederik wisely foresaw what would happen with no zoning laws so we concentrated on inland property but found nothing. A few hours before our plane was to leave for the mainland, a friend of Frank's showed up and assured us she'd found the perfect piece of land. Off we went again, with two hours to spare.

The land we were shown was remote, in the hills not far from the village of Santa Eulalia, and had a magnificent sweeping view of lush green fields, and beyond, the Mediterranean. We bought it, asking our friend to handle the details of the sale and write when they were complete.

We went back to Marbella, I to my twenty workmen finishing my parents-in-law's house, Frederik to packing his car for the drive to Morocco.

Being a mother, one can't help loving Spain. I know people talk of mistreated animals there, but certainly the children are more pampered and fussed over than in any place I can think of. My twenty workmen proved the best babysitters ever for Nicolas: he was given trowel and cement and played all day with bricks and sticks. Whenever you travel with children in Spain, you're treated like a queen and always greeted with special warmth. Restaurants never make you feel like an outcast.

Just after Frederik's return to Marbella, we were notified that we'd looked at the piece of Ibizincan land next to the one we had actually bought. We now also held title to its "improvements": the ruins of a large old farmhouse, a natural spring, a five-eighths interest in an olive mill, and an orange grove containing a 10x10-foot patch of weeds belonging to a Cuban whom we haven't yet found. The seclusion and the view were the same, and the thought of restoring an old house held far more appeal for me than building a new one.

The prospects of this restoration only enhanced the great feeling of *joie de vivre* I knew that summer. We had an endless stream of house guests. The workmen finally finished. I organized, cooked, sewed and never felt better on a daily regimen of much garlic, olive oil, gallons of wine and swims in the pool where I wore a bright pink, homemade bathing outfit—I looked like a giant living beach ball! Came end of July, and still no baby. Came August, and we went to the bullfights in Malaga every day, hoping the excitement would have its effects. But, all I did was nod and greet my doctor, who usually sat a few rows in front of us.

154

Frederik and I both became very impatient and nervous, as a September tour was growing uncomfortably close. One night after returning from the bullfights, he and I had one of our major arguments, about why the devil I couldn't give birth (I was nearly three weeks "overdue," if there is such a thing). Why couldn't I produce this child that wouldn't arrive, he raged. I countered that there wasn't anything I could do about it. His face became beet red with anger. I'd seen this often before, but now found myself in a situation similar to one which transpired five years ago. Now I was facing him alone with a glass of sherry in my hand. I threw it, expecting his face to sizzle—the laughter was bubbling inside me. I have this tendency to let my mind shift into total objectivity, see a situation in all its absurdity and feel an insuppressible desire to laugh. But one has to be sure the other party feels the same way. Five years ago, the argument had been just as ridiculous: Was Callas a nice person in private, or not? I insisted she couldn't sing like that without a beautiful soul; Frederik disagreed. Neither of us had ever met her, of course, and only knew what the papers said. The result of that bout was my accidentally putting his flat on fire, when in flight I dropped my cigarette. This time, mellowed by motherhood, I merely pricked his finger, but you'd have thought I'd cut his throat.

I hate arguments, have always abhorred them, and will go to extremes to avoid them. At times of conflict, all my Cancerian traits appear. I usually tune out and crawl into my crab shell, and if things get really bad, I disappear into "my hole in the sand" and wait till the storm blows over. With me always are two sayings of my mother's: "Never let the sun set on your wrath," which she learned from my father, and "Whatever you say in anger cannot be undone, so always remember that before you speak."

The evening of August 8, 1963, I quietly packed my suitcase and started my natural childbirth breathing exercises without letting on. By six the next morning, I figured things were getting a bit close and woke Frederik. While I huffed and puffed in the car, he drove full speed to the clinic in Malaga, arriving at 8:00 A.M. on the nose, not a minute too early. At

155

8:09, barely out of my clothes and on to the delivery table, my second child was born.

Her birth was an unbelievable experience. Friends of Frederik told me later of the color and light sensations which LSD can provide. Although I've never tried LSD, childbirth apparently produced in a natural way a "trip" of its own for me. I had two breaths of gas. As the pain grew less, I seemed to look into an incredible warm yellow light which became whiter and brighter as I was lifted and floated, slowly spinning, upward. My body stretched, expanded and dissolved into this now unbearable but beautiful blinding white light. An explosion— a death. It was as if, in one split second, I was totally part of the universe. In the next instant I heard a cry, *"Es una nina!"* the doctor said.

By 9:00 A.M., I'd had a breakfast of croissants, scrambled eggs and coffee and my first cigarette. In Spain, a child must be named within an hour of birth. This we were not prepared for, especially since we'd never considered even the remotest possibility of having a daughter. Names of family and girl friends were discussed, but nothing clicked with both of us. The doctor was no help, anxiously popping his head through the door every ten minutes to announce the time and ask about results. The middle names (Clara, after my mother and Frederik's sister, and Eleanora) were easy choices. Perhaps by carrying the names of people we loved and admired very much—Eleanora was for Nora Élé and my godmother, Princess Viggo—the baby might assimilate some of their qualities. At last we agreed upon a first name: Kirsa, for my maternal grandmother. As it turned out, my grandmother had been christened "Kirstin," nicknaming herself Kirsa as a child, but "Kirsa" our Kirsa was.

I spent the next two-and-a-half days looking after Kirsa and enjoying a constant stream of visitors, mainly the families of all the other newborns there. They'd just make the rounds while visiting their own relatives, knocking on the door to see how my baby and I were doing. She stayed in the room with me (there also was a second bed for husband, mother or whoever) and was fed when she was hungry. These were moments of peace and lovely closeness.

156

I loved the atmosphere in the Malaga clinic. Every room overflowed at all hours with families, and friends old and young, rejoicing together over the new arrival. The Spanish approach to childbirth as a natural and happy event seemed so different from the sterile clinical approach I had experienced in Geneva—after all, one is not *ill* at such times. With my new "Leo-baby" in a basket, I happily burst from the clinic in three days and returned to Marbella. Frederik had flown ahead to Barcelona, hating long hot car trips, especially with the children. Five days later, I took off at 5:00 A.M. to join him, driving our dusty Buick station wagon with Nicolas, Nanny, baby and household gear loaded a yard high on the roof. It was a long haul. Whenever Kirsa had to be fed, I'd pull over to the edge of the road, sit in a ditch, and it was mealtime, while Nanny and Nicolas romped around picking flowers and chasing birds. Arriving at the Ritz in Madrid the same evening, all barefooted and grubby, we looked like a gypsy caravan. When I asked the desk manager how late the dining room would be open, he took one look and haughtily replied, "Madam, we have twenty-four hour room service!" I took the hint.

By next evening after another endless, sticky drive we were in Barcelona and then on to Puplinge where reluctantly we had to leave the children with the grandparents while we went on tour to Hong Kong and Australia.

Frederik had carefully arranged our flight on Air India so we could indulge in good curries instead of the usual airborne brown lettuce and rubbery chicken. Came Cairo, came Bombay—still no curry. What could we do? Finally we remembered there was a magic word: "Vegetarians!" we lied. With an "Ahhh" of understanding, the stewardess removed the chicken and brought what we wanted.

In Delhi we visited Frederik's sister and her husband and took a taxi through the Rajastan Desert with a maniacal Sikh driver. He leaned on both accelerator and horn for three solid days, doing a slalom through ox carts, children, chickens, bicyclists and sacred cows, and no amount of entreaty could make him slow down. I spent most of the time lying on the floor, expecting any minute to hear the crunch.

157

Outside of Delhi, a guide took us down to the sacred crypt and tomb of Agh Bar. Having carefully and reverently explained the extraordinary acoustics of the holy chambers, he let out the longest loudest belch I've ever heard, which bounced off the walls for at least two full minutes. So much for reverence! Frederik showed me all the sights he'd known when living there, and we flew on to Bangkok, to me the most delightful city in the Far East and with the most beautiful women (Frederik's always said he'd like to return to Bangkok alone, which I can fully understand!). The Thais have very close ties with Denmark, the Danes having established trading companies there at the same time as the British were colonizing India. The Danes, however, remained on a trading basis and quite a few Thais went to Denmark for their higher education. That the Thais have never been under western rule I find is very noticeable in their attitude and demeanor toward Europeans. There are none of the resentments or the contemptuous subservience one tends to find in other parts of the Orient, and the land's fertility and relative prosperity seem reflected in the always smiling Thai faces. But there was work to be done, and off we went to Hong Kong whose commercialism, after Bangkok, was a disappointment. We stayed and worked at the just-opened Mandarin, the first big-name attraction in their nightclub. Our audiences were predominantly Chinese who had the habit, perhaps stemming from the Chinese operas, of talking all through our act—most disconcerting, but one does adjust. We'd been assigned a room valet who, in his zeal to please, spread my nightgown on my bed and my large stage petticoat on Frederik's, both neatly pinched at the waist. . . . "So he's got *that* kind of a night-shirt," he probably figured.

In Australia, we were booked to do nightclubs in Sydney and Melbourne, but had problems with our contract. It had never been signed, and was always being returned to us with a new clause added. The Australian impresario had the advantage of being able to say, "Call your lawyer" (who was twelve thousand miles away) or "You can always go home" (the air fare was at least five hundred pounds). In all fairness, we

158

finally did sort out the contract, had great audiences and didn't have any difficulties on subsequent tours. The Australian liquor license laws do create certain problems, namely getting as much under one's belt as one can during drinking hours (that problem would never have existed had Australia been colonized by the French!). This situation accounted for a good-humored but sometimes noisy audience. One night, a particularly loud-mouthed gentleman was put down beautifully by a fellow customer with, "Throw the bloody sheep farmer out!" There wasn't another sound.

After two months we were going home again, and the closer we got to Geneva, the more unbearable my longing to see the children became. We were flying Qantas this time, having completely forgotten the curry flap on the way out, and now experienced the proof-positive of the airline's much-touted efficiency. The smells of kangaroo soup, hot turkey and all the trimmings wafted by as the stewardesses delivered their trays. But when our turn came, it was celery soup, fried potatoes and three kinds of dreary, droopy vegetables. We sat there like two giant question marks. Our fib over Bombay had come home to roost! The stewardess said sweetly, "We know you're vegetarians, sir, so we got this specially for you." It broke us up completely. No one around us could understand what they'd put into the potatoes to make us laugh so, and potatoes it was, all the way home.

Mid-November again saw me packing suitcases after a short break in Geneva. This time, Nanny and the children were coming, too. Over the next few years, we took the children with us everywhere except on tours of one-night stands. A lot of people have asked me how it's possible to trek around the world with young children without making them feel insecure and unstable. Looking at them today, I feel I've coped with that problem quite well. My first rule from the day Nicolas was born was that he'd always awaken to familiar faces—either his grandparents, Nanny, Frederik or me. I never used an outside babysitter anywhere. Also we never traveled without the children's own eiderdowns and pillows, their gaily printed sheets and cases, and all their favorite toys and animals. Besides that,

Nanny always had her "emergency bag" stuffed full of favorite cookies, baby food, diapers and, to my mother's horror, pacifiers. I know that pacifiers are considered unhygienic and most unattractive; however, if that gives *you* a good night's rest and the child a secure feeling, why not? Most dentists admit you'll save an awful lot of money in orthidonture that way, a pacifier being much less damaging to a child's bite than his own thumb (and a thumb is much harder to discard).

Whenever we checked into a new hotel, the children's needs were seen to first. Their things were immediately unpacked to create a sense of the familiar, and their routines set. I always tried to make each new hotel an adventure, showing them the small but special features of their suite. Only after all this was satisfactorily organized did I unpack our own things.

The Westbury where we stayed while performing at the Savoy was to become our home in London for many years. Nicolas immediately went to work on the affection of the Spanish maids. The hall porters, the bellmen and especially the lift man became great favorites as the children grew older.

Two memorable things happened while we were at the Savoy. The first was the assassination of President Kennedy, which we learned from the evening news. Absolutely stunned, we sat glued to the television set, completely forgetting to dress and make up for the show. Eventually we phoned the Savoy to see if the show had been canceled and got a rather astounding answer, "The show is on, but no political stuff tonight." We changed our repertoire that evening, as we found it impossible not to express our feelings. Somehow it was obvious from the audience reaction that most people hadn't heard the awful news and were slightly puzzled. Not until walking through the lobby after we'd finished did we see groups of people with newspapers talking in hushed voices. Everybody was as shocked as we were. Not since the end of the war can I remember an event which caused such an emotional reaction everywhere in Europe. A few days later we lunched with friends from California, and of course the conversation turned to the tragedy. They told us how they and their friends had celebrated the event with champagne! Immediately, Frederik put down the menu, we walked out, and we haven't seen them since.

The other event was of less worldly consequence, but to my world it brought changes. Frederik had always dreamed of owning a boat. Like me, he'd done a lot of sailing in his youth and, like most young couples, we'd always had the romantic notion of sailing around the world. That notion, of course, never includes financial limitations, storms, children and other trifles. At 4:00 A.M. over watercress sandwiches and well-mellowed with wine, he suddenly produced a huge photograph of the fifty-seven-foot ketch, *Sinbad,* he had just bought. I knew he'd been looking at the boat, but he'd solemnly promised he wouldn't buy it. Having just six months before bought the house in Ibiza, which was to be our summer retreat and place of retirement, our immediate need in my opinion was a flat of our own somewhere—*anywhere*—but in an area convenient to our work. I'd had enough of suitcases, and possessions scattered and stored with friends and family everywhere. Now, I saw my pots and pans and long-dreamed-of permanent cupboards sinking under the waves. There was no way we could afford both boat and flat. Frederik's timing for the announcement was perfect: I was too weary and too sick with disappointment to say anything. I knew I wouldn't be spending much time on the ketch because of the children, but then if that was what he wanted . . .

The boat was being repaired and fitted out in Denmark, and he wanted to sail it to Ibiza the following spring. My mother joined us for Christmas in Switzerland. Shortly afterward, Frederik went to Copenhagen to supervise work on the boat, leaving me once again to haul out the suitcases, this time to drive with Nanny and the children to Ibiza. Frederik was not very fond of anything that had to do with manual labor and home practicalities, and I was of the old-fashioned, firm and well-entrenched belief that a good housewife should save her husband from all the chores he didn't like. I enjoyed looking after his wishes and wants, but I felt very lonely.

Ibiza

We drove the car to Barcelona to take the weekly boat to Ibiza. The island was as lovely as I remembered it. Our own house couldn't be touched yet as there was a tenant farmer living in its two front rooms, and by Ibizincan custom he had a period of grace till the holiday of San Juan in mid-summer to get out. We moved into a small bungalow in Talamanca. At that time of year, April, Talamanca was a small collection of empty summer villas, plus a few houses belonging to locals, with a magnificent view across the bay of Ibiza Town. There were more stray dogs than people, so it was a bit quiet until "The Day of The Great Chicken Cleaning."

I'd dealt with chickens before, but never one still sporting its feathers, feet, head and innards. What a revolting mess! I stood near the kitchen window and tried to pull out the slimy entrails and cut off the bird's head without throwing up, then finally pitched the chicken against the wall and let out the most graphic four-letter English word I knew. Came a gentle voice from the balcony across the road, "Is there anything I can help you with?"

It was Herbert Burkholz, an American writer who lived with his wife, Susan, in a two-bedroom flat across the way.

162

They were drinking dry martinis, not my favorite drink, but I gratefully accepted one while Herb retrieved and cleaned the chicken.

Herb helped me wire the terrace to keep the kids from falling off, making me feel as though I were living in an enormous chicken coop. We all celebrated a delayed (or early) Thanksgiving together. Somehow, he'd come upon a turkey, a rarity in Ibiza, and some corn-on-the-cob (not the sweet kind, but the variety used for feeding hogs). Although the turkey was the toughest bird one could imagine, the corn as hard as a platter of cannonballs, and the gallons of wine not far from rotgut, it was a memorable evening.

Herb and Susan, like me, had arrived in Ibiza hardly knowing a soul. In fact, they had never been to Europe at all but had heard of Ibiza and just decided that's where he should work as a full-time writer. In the isolation of Talamanca, we found each other and have stuck together ever since.

My only other neighbors were the Botellas, who also became my friends. They'd come to the island in the '40's, had started a business and bought property. They had been married for twenty-seven years, had two grown daughters, but were still like newlyweds. I used to see them from my window in the evening, sitting on their terrace with drinks and holding hands. Then they'd turn on the gramophone and dance cheek-to-cheek in the moonlight. Sadly, they have both died since, and within a short time of each other.

A few weeks after I arrived I was invited on my first outing to explore some caves in the north of the island and later, on the beach, found myself sitting next to an attractive American who had earlier been introduced as a writer, Clifford Irving. My first impression was that, in size, he reminded me of the football players I'd known at the University of Southern California. And, I can't ever recall having seen a bigger pair of feet! Clifford, I found, was separated from his third wife, Fay, and with his son in great need of a playmate, asked if I'd bring Nicolas over the next day. I agreed. The next afternoon we drove to his house near Santa Eulalia, but he wasn't there, so

I left the two boys to get acquainted under the care of his housekeeper.

My return trip at dusk, however, produced Clifford, a short chat over a glass of wine on his terrace, and an invitation for dinner the next evening.

We met at Sandy's, one of the island's few bars. Its proprietor has an incredible memory for names and stories and is one of the most amusing, well-read people I know. In a way, Sandy personifies the complex function of Ibiza's bars: not just dispensers of food and drink, but the nerve centers of its social life. They serve as meeting places, message drops (only now are private phones beginning to appear—I won't have one), social centers, lost-and-founds—for things *and* people—and are really the glue that keeps the island's restless international crowd stuck together.

We had drinks, chatting with people we knew there, then Clifford suggested we go into Ibiza Town for dinner. In those days, there were few restaurants in Ibiza, and because the only sources of food were island produce and livestock, plus seafood, of course, the menu offerings and combinations were fairly limited: green salad with oil and vinegar, French fries, a broiled rabbit spread-eagled on a platter and looking as though he were about to leap off the table, tortillas of every sort, fish simply prepared but always extremely fresh, and chicken—everything fried in the same fat. As for meat, one of the most popular dishes was beef stew, only because the local cattle were so tough and stringy that stewing was a must.

Two spots in particular had their own quirks to add to the culinary interest. The first was the island's only exotic spot, an Indochinese place in a barnlike garage. There was no floor, just turf, long wooden tables and benches, and a flimsy partition separating the diners from the kitchen and the loo. In fact, the loo was smack in the middle of the dining room.

Juanito's is less exotic in food but boasts a splendid location: right on the harbor and also right on top of the town sewers, which are covered merely with an open grillwork and, in midsummer, cannot possibly be ignored. Nevertheless, it is and always has been a favorite of the foreign group, a place where one can linger over a glass of wine for hours and not be bothered. However, we chose neither of these, though I can't for the life of me remember where we did end up. We ate, drank wine and talked and talked and talked. Clifford was the first man in years who had paid me a compliment, not to the show-business me but just to *me* and that certainly registered. Much later, we discussed and laughed over that first date. Nothing was really said—only polite, amusing conversation—but we both were very much aware of each other.

We later went for a stroll on the pier, and Clifford regaled me with stories of the Ibiza he had known, having first arrived there in 1953. Nearly everyone on Ibiza had nicknames then, some still do: Hetty on the Jetty, a girl who sold fish soup on the pier; Mattress-Back Peggy; Deaf Henry; Poor Dead John, who got his name only after he'd died; Wanted John and many others.

The names were like a cast of players, Ibiza the stage. The players were real people creating, or re-creating, their very special fantasies from day to day. The stage encouraged complete acceptance of whatever one chose to be—or really was in the masquerade of the outside world—and no questions asked. All the players were beautiful in their own and each other's eyes, fully reflecting the beauty of the stage, and this has only changed slowly.

We walked and talked a bit more, then parted. It had been a beautiful, timeless, suspended-in-space evening, one of the nicest I'd spent in years, but as I drove home, I found myself disturbed.

In the days that followed, we saw each other as often as possible: at the beach with our children and sometimes on our own, at parties given by mutual friends, at dinner a few times and at his studio in Old Town. It was there over late-night bottles of wine by candlelight that the conversation changed from the lighthearted and superficial to things philosophical and personal, and failures and dreams gone by. It was if all that had been damned up inside me for years was suddenly gushing forth like a spring stream swollen by the melting snows. We were unknown entities to each other and, in slowly discovering each other, discovered ourselves as well. Perhaps I should speak only for myself.

There was something in Clifford I had never before found in the very few men who had become important in my life. I think it was a blend of the curiously American qualities of openness, warmth and courtesy, of strength and basic optimism about life which are, perhaps, particularly attractive and intriguing to European women. Clifford gave me an extraordinary feeling of being protected—ironic, I know in retrospect —and yet, that's what I felt.

It was all such a revelation—I fell in love. Whether I'd fallen in love with love or was really in love, I didn't know and was greatly upset that things were getting totally beyond my control. I felt no guilt, rather a confused sensation of "What am I doing? What's going on?"

With Clifford I discovered and experienced Ibiza in all its magic—that was his gift to me. Our love remained on the airy-fairy level of a glance, a touch, an outstretched hand, a kiss . . . no more, for fear of breaking the spell. Somehow, I'd transferred to him the dream of the island I'd had for Frederik and me.

Two weeks later—or was it three—we were at the beach with the children. Glancing up, I spotted Frederik stalking down the sands searching for me. He wasn't due for at least three more weeks but because of bad weather and too-close quarters with an unknown crew not to his liking, he'd left the boat in Southampton and taken a plane. In one flash, as on a giant panoramic screen, the present was frozen crystal clear and completely in focus, and *I* had to push the button to make the reel go on. I couldn't take my sunglasses off as I greeted him. We packed up the kids, and went home. The reel had started moving again. He knew something was wrong, and I told him. It was nothing I had wanted or willed. I loved him, I was in love with Clifford—one loves people on different planes.

Frederik was enraged and at the same time hurt, and his violent reaction surprised me. For so long, I'd really felt like a wind-up doll: it goes here, it goes there, it sits, stands, sings

166

and raises the children—and now and then it would be dusted and polished and shown off with possessive pleasure. The reaction now was the Frederik I loved and, oddly enough, it gave me hope.

As the evening wore on, the cold, hard realities of the whole thing slipped into perspective. Was this not another Ibiza fantasy of no tomorrows (I'd heard of so many)? With two babies, a complex but surely very special relationship with Frederik, and our families who loved us all, could I really jeopardize all this because of this feeling for a man who was, after all, a stranger—not so much anymore to me, of course, but to everything my life had been up to that point? I couldn't—I was suddenly sure I couldn't.

Frederik's fury gradually subsided. Later, he told me that at the time he was not so angry at my confusion as with my choice. Clifford, to his thinking, was worth no more than a dalliance, if anything.

Three days later, Clifford and I met and we had very little to say to each other. It was over—it had to be. That afternoon, Frederik agreed that I should go to Copenhagen for a week. I needed to get away and my old friend Bee was home on a visit, so I had the perfect excuse for being there without telling anyone the real reason why. When I returned to Ibiza eight days later, things were all right, as I had determined they would be. I saw Clifford several times again that summer of '64 at parties and around the island, but we hardly spoke to each other. It was as though we'd both turned off a switch. By late July Frederik and I were back in London in a rented house preparing our act for our opening at "Talk of The Town," one of London's leading nightclubs. The schedule I set myself was heavier than usual. Getting up with the children at 6:30 began my day. Then:

7:00   Made breakfast for the children, Nanny and my-
        self, then prepared stew or spaghetti or curry for
        the late night supper we'd have after the show,
        always with an unknown number of people. I then
        cleaned, got the laundry together and did the mar-

keting or whatever needed doing most on that particular day.

10:00   Rehearsed in the house with Frederik for the act or, after it opened, for a record we were to do that September and a concert tour.

1:00   Broke from rehearsal, making lunch for children, Nanny, my mother who visited for a few days, musicians, and anyone who'd popped by, and played with the children before their naps.

3:00   More rehearsals for the record and the tour.

5:00   Made supper for children, playing and chatting with them before baths and bed.

6:00   Tea and the TV evening news.

7:00   Bathed, washed and set hair.

9:30   Short rest, and make up for the show.

10:30   Left for "Talk of the Town," arriving well ahead of time to get our heads into doing the show.

Midnight The show began, lasting until 1:00 or 1:15, after which there'd be the usual throng of backstage visitors, business matters, rehashing of the performance and so on.

3:00   Back home, I'd serve the supper I'd made that morning to the ever-changing entourage, mostly new-found friends of Frederik's.

5:00   Mercifully, to bed, setting the alarm for 6:30 to begin again.

Rehearsals were gratifying but enervating. The household chores were left behind, and we were totally into the world of music. George Hall, now director of the Central School of Drama, was once again working with us as he'd done in previous years. As an artistic adviser and friend, he was invaluable and much of our success should be attributed to him. We always seemed to be blessed with finding people who, with infinite patience and understanding, would help us greatly. The cabaret ended, the recording ended, the concert tour ended, and I was very thin. It was time to pack the suitcases again: Paris, Geneva, Hamburg, Barcelona and finally all together on Ibiza.

168

Work had started on the farmhouse, but restoring it the way we had planned it would take at least another year. Frederik had rented a house sight unseen, except for a color layout of it that had caught his eye in *Maison et Jardin*. It had been built by two artist friends of mine with the help of a Boy Scout manual and a lot of taste and imagination.

The house was starkly Oriental, its spaciousness and proportions perfect. There was no conventional furniture but, in lieu of beds and chairs, cement benches with cushions of bright orange sack-cloth stuffed with dried seaweed. With no electricity and only dozens of candles to light the evening, it was lovely.

The practical side of life was another matter. Water had to be pumped from a well to the roof every single day. The water supply system was designed to use solar heat to warm things up—it rained steadily every day. Of *course* the roof leaked, and dozens of pots and bowls had to be placed to catch the inpouring. Late each night when the rain was worst, I had to sweep the library, still roofless, to keep it from flooding the bedrooms below. The plumbing was a mass of green garden hoses joined together on the roof like a giant octopus. The day the hoses jumped off their cistern spigots was a day to be remembered—it was the only real shower I had the whole time there. With the incessant wind, the doors had to be propped shut with rocks, and the newspapers stuffing the unfinished windows would come dancing through the room. The unusually low, small loos had their problems, too. Kirsa got stuck in one playing hide-and-seek, and the other could take no paper.

The kitchen was an adventure in itself. Because of scant storage space and lots of mice, we had to hang the food from the ceiling. The mice persisted, so I fed them every night, and watched in amusement their dancing shadows on the candlelit wall. The two leaky gas burners had to be lit at the tap as well or one would gas oneself cooking. The ultimate was the foot-deep, goldfish-filled pond outside the front door. Departing friends, especially after a glass or two of wine, would invariably walk straight into it in the darkness. Not a day went by that the kids didn't slosh around in it, too.

After a month, the fireplace collapsed, and a kerosene stove

169

was hauled in, not nearly so romantic but certainly needed and welcome. The house was so chilly and damp that all my home-made Christmas decorations, hung on the tree two nights before Christmas, were completely unglued by Christmas morning, nothing more than a huge pile of bits of straw, paper, and what-have-you. Still, the Christmas tree fetched from the mountains behind the house was one of the loveliest I've ever know, and we had one hundred and fifty people that evening for hot gløg and smørrebrød. It was a great party lasting from 6:00 P.M. to 6:00 A.M., at which point I found myself on all fours with a can of Ajax scrubbing wine stains from the very porous Spanish tile floors.

Frederik spent most of his time in Ibiza Town. Sometimes he would bring friends home, but whenever I joined them, I felt unwelcome, intruding and uncomfortable. He had be-come very distant, remote and strange.

Late in January, we did two weeks in Monte Carlo in the Casino's nightclub. There were very few people around, a bit like a ghost town. In the quiet, the rhythm of the old world atmosphere of Russian Grand Dukes and caviar seemed to breathe again. It was a restful time, and never has a dry warm bed with clean sheets been more appreciated than after the madness of Ibiza. On long walks exploring the town, I was especially struck by the displays of antique jewelry in some of the shop windows—so many of the beautiful pieces surely had a tale to tell.

Spring, 1965, found us flying to Australia and New Zea-land, this time with Nanny and children. We broke the trip in Hong Kong for two days, thinking we would show the chil-dren the sights. Our success was not without flaws. Kirsa, twenty months old, instantly fell in love with the Sikh door-man at the Mandarin Hotel where we stayed, and refused to leave his side. And, being presented with shark fin soup, she spent a good half-hour methodically spitting out every bit of fin. She escaped our surveillance at every possible oppor-tunity, presumably to rejoin her true love in the lobby. On one occasion she disappeared into the automatic lift. As the elec-tronic doors closed, I could hear her peal of laughter coming up the shaft. For one split second, I considered running down the twenty-two flights of stairs, but thought better of it. I was terrified she'd be squashed in one of the doors on the way down. Not at all! She was on her way out the front door to rejoin her Sikh by the time I'd gotten down in the next lift.

Nicolas was his lovely, gentle, nearly four-year-old self. The Star Ferry to Kowloon was heavily supported by us for two days as we made trips backward and forward, backward and forward. In Sydney we enrolled them in a nursery school whose barrels and swings and slides held far more fascination than all the kangaroos and bell birds of Australia. After five weeks of work there, we sent Nanny and the children home and went on to New Zealand to do a grueling schedule of one-night stands. By now I knew I was pregnant again, and by early June was grateful for my Empire gowns. By walking in a straight line downstage, always facing front and backing off the same way I'd come, I avoided being seen in profile: in those days, it still wasn't acceptable to appear on stage pregnant. The minute we returned to Geneva, I exhaled for the first time in weeks and my girth immediately increased by a good ten inches.

Once again, we'd blocked out a vacation period in our schedule, but somehow, I never could keep our professional calendar and my child-bearing schedules straight, so long-awaited holidays invariably found me waddling into or tottering out of one clinic or another. Nanny went on a much-deserved long vacation, and the children and I left for Ibiza. I was bone tired and not well at all.

The tourist boom was just hitting Ibiza in '65. I lived in three unfinished hotels and then figured if I were going to stay anywhere, it might as well be in my own shell of a home. Frederik, arriving shortly after, had stayed with friends in town and then gone off on the *Sinbad*. During that spring, he had become very remote indeed. I knew he was deep into Sufism, but his esoteric studies removed him from me rather than bringing us closer. Most of the students of mysticism I had encountered at that point seemed totally preoccupied with their inner selves to the exclusion of all others around them.

171

They gave one the feeling that anybody who was not searching on the same "trip" was a loss and a write-off. I knew Frederik's restlessness had not been spawned by boredom, but was nurtured by his seeking and searching. He had to experiment and experience. I understood it and yet I didn't, and I didn't know how to live with it.

My mother had visited briefly while I agonized through a case of food poisoning, but now I was once more left alone with the children. The heat that summer was insufferable. We had very little furniture in the house, no electricity, the water at first had to be fetched from the spring below, and the children were irritable and whiny and wanted constant attention.

The house was full of dirt, cement bricks, workmen, packing crates and bugs, not necessarily in that order, plus a million or so fleas and flies who apparently decided to spice up their diet and go Danish. Again, I threw myself into the chores at hand—arguing with the workers, mixing paints myself, digging up missing sinks and fixtures, harassing the local shopkeepers and constantly stalking the plumber by parking myself on his doorstep in order to corner him on his return from God-knows-where at lunch or dinner.

By the end of summer, I was emotionally and physically at an all-time low. Frederik turned up a few times to see how things were getting on, but he now lived in a different world and communication had broken down altogether. As I dragged myself off to bed at night, having doused the children and myself with vinegar to ease the itching of the flea bites, the baby began her gymnastics and kept me awake until dawn. I cried a lot then. Slowly, she and I had developed a pact: I'd live to get her born but I really didn't want to go on afterward.

I'd considered for a while having the baby in the small Ibiza clinic, but rejected that idea because of my good memories of my previous stay in the clinic in Malaga. A week before the baby was due, we moved to a hotel there (Frederik and Frank had arrived home from their cruise), but this time there were no bullfights and very little merriment. After four unbearably long weeks, I pleaded with the doctor to induce the birth. He

172

agreed, gave me the necessary shots and, within two hours, I was once again on the delivery table. But this time it was a nightmare. I started spinning faster and faster as darkness closed in, a darkness so stifling that it was almost touchable, and I looked down into a whirlpool drawing me down and down into its vortex. I felt as though my whole being was disintegrating, as if my mind had left my body and everything had become separated. The fear was unbearable. I had an indescribable feeling of having lost all control, I fainted and Ana Maria was born. It was just noon.

The pain and hemorrhaging continued all afternoon. Blood was brought in, but my veins were so collaspsed it took several minutes to find one. With an incredible machine that looked like a home chemistry set, they began pumping ice-cold blood (straight from the refrigerator) into my arm at such a rate that it took only seven minutes to empty the pint bottle. My arm turned to a piece of ice and lost all feeling—it was kind of eerie, like lying in bed with someone else's arm.

The next day it was still going on, and they decided to give me penicillin. It never occurred to anyone that the real problem was the afterbirth.

After a few days of penicillin, and two operations without anesthethic, I went into cardiac failure. A hastily summoned heart specialist threw out the penicillin and used other medication to get my heart back to normal.

Just after that, my mother arrived. Frederik had not even told the family what was going on, only that we'd had a daughter, eight pounds, doing fine.

After two weeks of this medical nightmare, I was told I was to do a radio interview. The excited nuns propped me up with beautifully embroidered sheets and pillows and somehow concealed the fact that the glamorous "artista's" awful matted hair hadn't seen a comb for a fortnight. How I got my Spanish together, I'll never know (and maybe I didn't), but the interview was okay and mercifully brief. Immediately after, the nuns came racing in to cart out the sheets and pillows and get back to the business of keeping me alive.

The nuns were gentle, kind and always smiling, and during

my very bad nights would stay on their own time watching over me while saying their Rosary. The doctor was terribly concerned. Both he and his wife would visit me at all hours of night and day, and on Sunday mornings, everyone would go to services in the chapel downstairs. By this time I really wanted their prayers to work!

In the beginning I had seen very little of Ana Maria, but now she was rolled in every day for short periods so that she could be with me, though I still couldn't take care of her myself.

It was my mother who attended to her needs, who also read to me daily, and some nights slept in the other bed—she was altogether wonderful. She and Frederik quickly agreed when I insisted: "Get me back to Switzerland. . . . I want to see my kids."

Nineteen days after my confinement, Mother, Ana Maria in a basket and I, shuffling like an old lady, got on a plane for Geneva, where I was immediately sent to another clinic by our family doctor.

In the convalescent home that night, all hell broke loose. I didn't know what had happened, but I thought all my insides had come out and I was about to die. The gynecologist was finally located at 2:00 A.M. and moved me to his clinic for surgery. At last, the afterbirth . . . which he presented to me later in a pickle jar! Enraged at what had happened to me, he could only repeat, "You've got to sue, you've got to sue!"

I spent nearly three weeks in that clinic, building up my strength with French food and wine of Cordon Bleu standards. What bliss, were all hospital food so carefully and delectably prepared! The day I was discharged, my doctor told me he was writing the entire episode as a case history for use in the university's medical school. As far as I know, my anonymous but minutely detailed innards are still entertaining the gynecological students.

After six weeks within the confines of one medical facility or another, it was awfully good to be home and with the children again. My mother-in-law went to no end of trouble cooking special foods and surrounding me with flowers and quiet. It took two months before I could walk up the stairs and when, finally, I slowly and shakily made it to the top, she stood there and hugged me. We became very close.

When I was at last able to pick up Ana Maria and carry her around, she decided not to let go or let me out of her sight, and that lasted for years. As long as she was in her little basket in the same room with me, she was quiet. As she grew, I used to tote her everywhere slung over one hip and, to this day, she still needs the physical contact.

It's strange how the children's personalities reflect not only their astrological signs but the circumstances and my emotions at the times of their births. Floris Nicolas Ali, the Gemini, is a gentle soul, a little shy but very loving, absentminded, interested in things scientific and mechanical. He expresses his humor endlessly in drawings and cartoons, has never told a lie, likes being on his own and reads avidly. Kirsa Eleonora Clara, the Leo, is extroverted, a clown with great talent for mimicry, a beautiful large singing voice, athletically built, practical and with instant emotions. Ana Maria Else, the Scorpio, is an old soul, stubborn, determined and intuitive. She's fine-boned, long and slender and slightly awkward. She reasons and argues until she has her way, and she constantly needs to express her love by touch.

Children are mystical little beings who, one day, arrive into your world, painfully, joyfully, full of secrets, and then depart with most of those secrets still intact. You catch glimpses of those secrets and love your children as you protect and watch them grow, only to reach out and find them disappearing into the morning mist.

Ana Maria was christened that Christmas—as Kirsa had been—by Murshid Mushrafan, who was now head of the Sufi movement. Frederik had wanted to bring Murshid Ali Khan to Denmark to christen Nicolas years before, but suspecting what the reaction there to an Indian mystic in yellow robes would have been, I vehemently argued against it and won. Besides, I could not think of my firstborn's not being christened in our own traditional way.

175

"Deine Liebe mag sein..."

Frederik preceded us to London from Puplinge. We'd decided to rent a flat this time, as
we'd be spending three months there. By the time I joined
him, it was the first of February, 1966, and I went straight into
rehearsals. I was terribly tired and depressed all the time, and
tears would flow uncontrollably at the slightest provocation.
This made the rehearsals very trying and intensified the arguments Frederik and I always did have over our work. We were
two individuals with very definite ideas of what we wanted to
do, yet, we had an agreement that he should have the final say.
We did interviews, radio and TV, and toured up and down
England doing one-night stands and ended up in Albert Hall.

I'd never been to Albert Hall, and walking in for a rehearsal
that afternoon, I froze. To me, it was a giant ampitheatre and
I was about to be thrown to the lions. Frank Willoughby, our
regular pianist, was with us that night, his wife, a close friend
too, stood in the wings like a living good-luck charm. That
evening was the zenith of our career. The place was sold out
—6,900 seats and all the standing room—and only one seat
ticket hadn't been picked up. As we entered to a cascade of
applause from all sides, including the seats behind us on stage,
my knees began shaking uncontrollably and shook for the next

176

five minutes. The emotion of the moment constricted my throat as I fought back the tears. We'd finally achieved what we'd talked about for so long: to be alone on stage for a whole evening in one of the most revered halls in Europe. The evening flew, ending before we knew it, but the delicious lightheadedness, like a high from champagne, stayed with us and the musicians for the next two or three days. Always before, I'd relived a performance in bed, scrutinizing, criticizing, trying to figure what had worked and what hadn't so as to improve the next performance. This time *everything* had worked, and for once my self-criticism couldn't destroy my joy. Our repertoire by now had grown to encompass songs from musicals, contemporary folk songs, protest songs (we never believed in hitting people over the head, but rather, in holding up a mirror subtly and humorously to reflect the wrongs and the ills of the times) and, of course, some of Frederik's own music.

Summer brought what was becoming our annual separation: Frederik was off on his boat, I stayed in the house in Ibiza with the children. Despite my great loneliness without him, the house was really taking shape. Flea-free at last, it had begun to regain its long-buried charm and beauty.

I saw a few old friends again, among them David Walsh, who much later would have an unwitting part in the Hughes affair through some watercolors of Hughes commissioned by Clifford. There was Elmyr de Hory, who surprised us all when it was later revealed that his paintings in the style of various impressionists had been sold all over the world. None of us had known that Elmyr even dabbled in painting, let alone had the talent to fool the experts. To us, he had always been a patron of the arts helping young artists who needed money or had talent worth encouraging. Ever charming, he was and still is a wonderful host, excellent cook and one of the most amusing raconteurs I know. Frank visited us, but in the evenings Nanny and I were left to our own devices, sewing, painting, repairing. Over the years I've become no mean handyman!

And, of course, there was Clifford Irving. Our only contact in the two years since our parting had been one sympathetic letter from him sent that spring when he'd heard I'd been ill. He'd divorced Fay and had been living, on and off, with a German girl named Edith, whom he'd known for some time.

We ran into each other at the beach one day, and he asked me to come by his studio for a glass of wine. A day or so later, I did. I hadn't heard much from Frederik that summer: he was still off sailing with his friends. Our relationship was disintegrating rapidly, and although we loved each other, it was as if we were constantly getting our wires crossed. I suppose I had my rigid ideas of what marriage should be, and I'd come to realize that basically Frederik didn't want to be married at all. I understood his restlessness and searching, but felt left out of his inner world and very unhappy. We were, perhaps, just too different to stay together. I became brittle and defiant that summer.

Clifford and I, trying to recapture a happier time, were soon woven into the spell of the island and began seeing each other again, just the two of us alone. During the afternoons we could steal, we swam off the rocks below his studio, drank wine on his terrace or in the clutter of his paper-strewn workroom, listened to music, talked or argued, and pretended that time didn't exist—no past, no future, a very common phenomenon in Ibiza. That summer, we were lovers.

But at the end of July, when I had to leave to go back to work, we realized there was a curfew even in never-neverland. We both wondered whether our feelings for each other could survive in the real world outside or whether our relationship was simple and pure only because it had never been exposed to the frictions and humdrum of everyday life. We decided before I left to try and see each other sometime that winter.

Frederik came and we returned to London and started packing for yet another tour of Australia and New Zealand, lasting through September and October. We were friends and we even talked about the feasibility of working together and living apart, but that to me seemed impossible. Our private lives and career were so much of a whole that I felt to separate even partially just wouldn't work. During the tour, he told me he

178

had met someone during the summer. I didn't realize at the time how radically this girl would affect our lives.

The tour "Down Under" was extremely successful, but very tiring. It mostly consisted of one-night stands, except for the major towns. In Wellington, New Zealand, the Governor-General, Sir Bernard and Lady Ferguson, old friends of my mother's, had most hospitably invited us to stay at Government House. One gets so weary of hotels—they more and more resemble each other—so this was a real treat. We had a wonderful time there, and the Fergusons came to the black-tie opening night. As "The Queen . . ." was solemnly played and the Governor-General was standing resplendent in his uniform, the first drops of rain came through the roof. The first landed on my nose, the next on Frederik's guitar, another trickled down his beard. As the last notes died away, we were quietly fidgeting in place, trying not to move our feet or bodies but still hoping to duck the constant stream from the roof now forming a puddle in front of us on the stage. They had warned us it rained a lot in Wellington, but this was ridiculous!

During the third song the mike gave out. We learned later that the sound man was off somewhere for the evening and had sent a substitute who didn't know which knob was which, let alone how to twiddle them. After various attempts at defying the sound system, Frederik finally stomped off in a rage and I switched into one of my sweet gentle solos. As the vocabulary from the wings grew louder and stronger, I had to sing louder and louder in order to keep the illusion going. Just short of mayhem and murder backstage (and utter absurdity on stage), the sound was fixed and we finished the show.

We witnessed in Wellington an old Maori chieftain's recording in sing-song voice the names of his forefathers all the way back to the landing of the first canoe on the island hundreds of years before. This recitation was usually part of the ritual for initiation into manhood, which he'd undergone more than a half-century earlier.

What New Zealand lacks in social contact and stimulation, it more than makes up for in the beauty and variety of its

179

natural resources. When you drive through the countryside, the green hills look as though they're overgrown with white wooly mushrooms. As you get nearer, you discover they have heads and tails and say "Baaaaa. . . ."

At the time of our tours, there was very little television, and it was a joy to find people so theatre-going and theatre-minded. Too, I've never come across so many bookstores anywhere in the world.

Back to Geneva in a state of total exhaustion, we decided to take a break for Christmas from each other. I left for Antigua with the children and Nanny, accepting a long-standing invitation to visit Bee and her husband, who lived in Boston with their three children but had a lovely winter home in Mill Reef.

Frederik went to Ibiza.

We stayed two-and-a-half months at Mill Reef. Diving with aqualungs, I found a sort of peace I'd not known since childhood. The silence and weightlessness beneath the sea produces the most exhilarating feeling, and the colors are incredibly beautiful. All movement seems unreal in its softness and slowness. Looking through the water, you get an unbelievable sense of infinity. I guess it's the same sensation of free spirit people experience when they sail out on the ocean or reach the peak of a great mountain. Could I have been "be-gilled" by some magical process, I'd have just stayed down there and never come up. Suddenly I understood mermaids.

Needless to say, the children loved the beach. Christmas Eve, 1966, was sweated out under a tropical sky amidst the slightly bizarre chaos of mountains of multicolored packages, plastic Santa Clauses, Christmas stockings, screeching children and strong support for the frazzled parents from rum punch. It was all so lovely and yet, despite its tropical splendor, it just couldn't compare with Ibiza.

Sometime in January, tanned, with hair well-bleached by the sun, we got out our winter clothes and started the trip home. Clifford had written that he'd be in New York on business, so en route we stopped there for a few days and we met. The meeting was a disaster. Clifford's writing wasn't going very well and he was depressed. As for me, by the end of my stay at Mill Reef, I was missing Frederik and longing to get home. Clifford and I really had nothing to say to each other. Perhaps the love between us could flourish only in Ibiza after all. I know both of us were privately relieved when the plane took off for London.

When we arrived at Heathrow, my heart as always skipped a beat seeing Frederik in the airport, and my hopes were high. I had a new determination to somehow right things between us. We had found another flat to rent, and Nicolas and Frederik went off to Ibiza while Nanny, the two girls and I coped with the mess of moving in. We wanted to have everything ready for their return and, working around the clock, we did it. One month later, I opened the door to the two of them and said, "Welcome home!"

A few days afterward Nicolas was sampling a cake I'd just made.

"It's very good, Mummy, but not as good as Dorothy's."

"Who's Dorothy?"

"Daddy's friend who was with us in Ibiza just now."

I never mentioned the cake incident to Frederik, determined to forget it. Three weeks later, after a dinner party, he suddenly sat up in bed and said, "Dorothy and I are expecting a baby. Our marriage is finished. It was only an extension of our childhood anyway, and only our work has held us together. We'll fulfill the contracts we have, and that's the end."

What could I say? I, too, had contemplated leaving but had come to a different conclusion. I had long known of his girl friends, but had come to terms with that. I knew what we had together was unique—and giving life together was very much a part of it. Now, with *this,* part of that uniqueness had been sullied and it all seemed meaningless. I was numb.

I cried and raged, then pulled on some clothes and wandered along the Thames till dawn. After coming back, I sat in the study staring at the wall. Later I called my mother-in-law in Holland. I knew she had enough love for both of us to be impartial in helping us if we wanted help—and I did. She said she'd come at once.

181

Meanwhile, we had a show to do that night. I'd been ill on the boards before, both in spirit and body, but nothing like this. I became a crab again, doing my grateful dance well-hidden in my shell. My mother's old-world self-discipline held up. Nobody knew. My mother-in-law's advice was "Love and patience, and you'll always win. Don't leave him!" I never had wanted to leave him, and I didn't then. I had always been in love with an ideal I saw in him. I couldn't stand watching him waste his time when I knew the potential was there and all he had to do was reach for it. Maybe that's what all women are in love with in their men—I don't know. Maybe we're all fictions of each others' imaginations. But then, sometimes this fiction must become reality. How else can lovers persist in being each other's conscience if it weren't for goading that ideal into fulfillment? What happened next, I do not know, I don't remember. The sun rose and the sun set and the whole world turned on its axis, and days turned into nights and nights into days. And I became like my dishwasher. I functioned.

We had a seven-week season in Brighton to do. With Frank as stage manager, we put the show together ourselves (there were two opening acts and the last half was ours), commuting from London every afternoon to return around two the next morning. On Sunday mornings, I'd bid Frederik farewell on his five-mile journey to Kensington, only to see him again Monday afternoon half-an-hour before train time. I cooked, I baked, I sewed, I played with the children—and inside I died a little more each day.

Yet, sometimes I could only laugh.

"How long do carrots have to cook?" he phoned.

"What do you do for morning sickness?"

"I just can't make the vacuum cleaner work!"

Frederik, who had never peeled a potato, let alone wielded a duster or changed a diaper in his life, was becoming domesticated. . . . As the months went by, his telephoned questions became more urgent: "Please make me a list for a layette . . ." My instant reaction was: "Oh my God, how can she not know *that?*" Then, "Goddamnitall!" And then . . . "Well,

182

you'll need twenty-four diapers, plenty of rubber pants . . ."

Directly from a charity performance at the Paris Opera, we went to Ibiza on our own. We were alone together for the first time in seven years. No work, no children, no family, no guests . . . all a bit belated. In a strange way our few days were like a beginning and an end. We laughed, we cried, we took long walks at sunset, sat on the terrace looking around us at the land we loved so much—and we loved each other very deeply. After three days, we returned to London.

At home the children never saw any strife or disharmony, but I know they sensed the tension. Children are extremely perceptive and direct. They see through all the walls we grown-ups seem to surround ourselves with in ever-widening circles. Frederik didn't want a divorce. I was his wife and would be the only one he'd have in this life. The soul relationship he had with Dorothy, he said, needed no marriage certificate.

He was torn between two worlds: when he was here, he wanted to be elsewhere; when elsewhere, he wanted to be here. Deep down I don't think he wanted to be anywhere. Then the phone rang: Dorothy had had a daughter. We both cried for each other, for ourselves, and for her, too.

We went on tour for six weeks late in '67. There were interviews to be given and songs to be sung, and we were "Nina and Frederik" to the world.

Came Christmas, there were toys and tinsel and a tree, and we sang carols to our children on BBC Television. Came spring, there were tulips, more travel and tours. We still had another year of contracts to fulfill. "You can have all we own then," he said. "Then" seemed so far, yet so frighteningly close. With "today" always as complicated as it was, I'd always comforted myself with the hope that "tomorrow" or "next year" would be better. We just have this engagement to finish, we just have that tour to do, and then . . . that had been going on for years, and suddenly the "tomorrow" was "then"—with no hope.

Frederik was prolific in his composing. His songs were totally esoteric in nature, the inspiration Dorothy, and I was

183

asked to help polish and perform them. I wish I'd known how not to suffer, for I understood them. More often than ever, he reminded me that—deeply irking to him—I was his conscience. It was like walking a rainbow of moods living with him . . . and *do* step gingerly on the purple.

When with us, he was a friend to me and the children, but it was funny how the little things hurt the most: for the first time in his life, he pushed a pram on Sundays in Hyde Park, just the three of them, like every other family on a Sunday afternoon.

One afternoon, I was packing my usual "care package" for Ibiza (tinfoil, dripless candles, Indonesian spices and such—my clothes were already there), when our travel agency phoned.

"Would you please tell Baron van Pallandt that his two tickets and hotel reservations for Morocco are in order? We weren't quite sure, though: does he want first class or economy?"

"Economy," I said in an uncharitable mood.

Sinbad had been sold, but I hadn't heard about Morocco. I'd hoped he'd spend the summer on Ibiza with the children and me, but that was not to be the case except for the first two weeks.

Once installed on the island Frederik brought friends home for dinner every night. As always, the conversations were of things philosophical, religious, esoteric and mystical, but the arguments, however vehement, never changed. I had listened for years but now lost my fear and patience and spoke up. To my surprise, I found I could beat them at their own game but then, intellectualizing is so easy.

Under the influence of a bit of everything, one dinner guest in a last desperate move of frustration got up and, banging his fist on the table, proclaimed, "I am God! I am God!" and stomped out. It just so happened the children walked in to say goodnight. For months after, they always greeted him with unusual reverence.

When Frederik left for Morocco, Eulalia started whitewashing the inside of the house. It should have been done much

184

earlier (late spring's the usual time), but we'd forgotten to let her know. Also, that winter had been very wet, and it took the walls a long time to dry. Eulalia first came to us from "across the hill." I couldn't quite see her that first day as she stepped through the kitchen door framed by the blinding sunlight, but as the curtain of long straw strings fell back again, I saw a round face with large brown laughing eyes. Her figure was clad in the high-waisted multi-skirted fashion of the peasants, with wide-sleeved blouse and tasseled shawl. The long black braid down her back was tied in the brightest cornflower-blue bow I've ever seen, and she carried a large straw hat. When she broke into a stream of Ibizincan, which I couldn't understand, it was as if the past had just walked through my doorway. She had such serenity and beauty that I could do nothing but ask her to sit down and have a cup of coffee. She'd come to work for me, sent by her uncle Nicholas, our tenant farmer. (Three years ago on a trip to the island, I was surprised and a bit saddened to see she'd joined the twentieth century: braid cut off, layers of skirts and the shawl discarded, clad now in a simple knee-length black dress—another milestone in the changes sweeping all of Ibiza.)

Farmer Nicholas also lives "across the hill" and comes to look after our land. He's a sinewy, gaunt man, tall for an Ibizincan, his age impossible to tell—when you work as hard as the farmers there do, you age very quickly, and he'd begun tending sheep when he was six. His grandchildren now play with my children among the olive trees, while he practices the flute sitting on one of the walls he's rebuilt. The art of fitting stone upon stone without mortar of any kind into a two-foot-thick wall which may run 50 to 100 feet is now a dying art. "You have to have an eye for the stone," an old man who used to help him would say. Nicholas knows of the "old ways."

The irrigation canals, just tumbled-down rubble ten years ago, are now brimming with water; the reservoir, always fed by a spring until the drought came, is once again full. We had to dig 320 feet to find water and had almost given up at 300 feet, but the water diviner was sure, so we kept going. I've tried one of those rods. Perhaps it was my imagination, but it worked.

Nicholas the farmer makes his own whitewash, or "cal" as they call it, and that's a dying art, too. Sometimes you can find a peeling wall and discover hundreds of layers of cal, each coating as thin as an onion skin, the whole thing at least an inch or more thick. Most of the island rock is limestone. Every three or four years, ten or twelve farmers get together with Nicholas for cal-making. I've seen this once, and it's like a ceremony, almost a ritual. A twelve-foot-high semi-circle has been cut out of the side of our hill. It's here that Nicholas stacks rock upon rock into a twelve-foot beehive-shaped structure, leaving a small opening in the bottom and a hollow flue to the top. Weeks beforehand, the farmers begin chopping wood and cleaning the brush from the tree-covered hills, bringing it all in piles to the "beehive" oven. To fire the stone takes approximately seventy-two hours, and the fire must be fed night and day to keep the temperature even. Each farmer has his hours of watch. During the day, there's usually just one or two on duty, but when night falls and the hours get long, the wives come with baskets of bread, wine, cold tortillas and sausage, and the flutes and drums begin. All night long, you hear the rhythm of their music echoing through the valleys and now and then the conch shell sounds to summon the next watch. Finally, the thin gray spiral smoke that's been curling up for three days turns white, and the firing is over. The oven is left to cool. When at last the outer layer of stones is removed, all the inner ones are snow-white, as if you'd taken the soot off the city snow and rediscovered its whiteness underneath. Each farmer gets his share of rocks to carry home, and for each year they're kept, the better the cal becomes.

At dawn I'd sit on my roof alone. Sunrise is my favorite time in Ibiza. There's a hush as the mist rises from the valleys and drifts away. The air is so clear and the light so extraordinary, as if a crystal lens has been placed before one's eyes, sharpening and intensifying the colors and images below. It's as though one is watching the very essence of awakening.

The weeks rushed by too swiftly as usual. The time came for

saying goodbye, and when the children hugged her as we left for London, Eualia cried as always.

Our next trip was again to Australia and New Zealand, and this time we took Frank Willoughby, our pianist, and his wife. It was a blur of one-night stands, and all I can remember were the air terminals, hotels and dressing rooms. I came alive only on stage.

That winter of '68 and spring of '69 back in London, I remember even less. Whenever in the house, Frederik enclosed himself in the study and demanded total silence: no music, no sounds from the children. My books collected dust. The silence was interrupted only by orders for tea and honey from the study. The sound of the doorbell or phone in this living tomb soon jarred every nerve in the body. I became a recluse and saw nobody except Frank Powis, who had become a kind of bridge between Frederik and me. The outside world became so frightening, I never left the flat.

Frederik announced he'd ordered a ten-meter catamaran to be delivered in the spring of '69. He planned to sail around the world, part of the way with friends and Dorothy, part of the way alone, and had carefully calculated all the modifications he would need to add to the standard Bobcat. It would be equipped in such a way that he could easily handle it alone. Every weekend he'd go to Southampton to check its progress and would come home full of enthusiasm. We made a list together of things necessary for living on board, and I scoured London and Copenhagen with painstaking care selecting every towel, sheet and dish. Everything was blue, including me. I sewed the curtains to match the tablecloth, knowing I'd never use any of it. Every stitch was a step closer to leave-taking.

In April, I loaded Nanny and the children into the car and drove to Ibiza. Frederik was sailing the boat down with Frank and a friend as crew. Ibiza was his first port-of-call on the voyage. I'd become completely detached and, in retrospect, had lost my grip. My love for the children was the only thing that kept me going. Frederik and I had talked of his moving his other family in with us in Ibiza, and I had wrestled with the problems of accepting and coping with that, but I really didn't know how we could do that. It seemed to me that if only I were out of the way, Frederik would be free to continue his life in a way meaningful to him, and all the children would be united with him. He would be at peace to write or compose and do whatever he might want to do. Our last album had been his own compositions of the past two years. For the jacket he'd chosen a striking color photograph of a lone seagull soaring against a limitless blue sky. That had deeply hurt me, for he'd long thought of the unfettered gull as his personal symbol. In endless walks around the countryside now, I decided how my struggles would end.

In those days, one didn't need a prescription to buy sleeping pills on Ibiza, and that seemed the neatest, most civilized way of doing it. I wrote a farewell note but tore it up. What's the point of leaving dramatic letters if you're not around to watch people's faces as they read them? Nanny was out and I'd sent the kids off with a friend for the weekend. I decided I would quietly sit on my terrace and take in the world for the last time, get terribly drunk, swallow the whole pile of pills, and just fade away. . . . I thought of the mystics' belief that you must die in order to live, and that one should do whatever one wanted regardless of the responsibilities one might have to ignore. I'd always argued violently that this was not possible, life was not that simple, especially if one had children (my friends supporting the "follow-your-soul" approach had none). But at this point, sitting on my terrace, I had completely come to terms with losing what I loved most, letting go of everything that meant anything to me at all. I had given up.

I sat there in my rocking chair looking out over the fields at the sea and suddenly realized there's absolutely nothing anyone could do to me, because I was totally devoid of fear, even of death. Anything anyone did to me, including taking my life, did not matter at all. I then figured, if that's true, what the devil am I doing taking my *own* life, which now seemed a despicable and selfish act. My feeling was one of total liberation, an incredible state of grace. After sitting for a long while,

I went up the hill and poured the whole batch of pills into the abandoned well.

When I got back to the house, I found an old friend had been by, drunk a glass of wine as was the local custom, and gone on. He'd left a message: a beautiful photograph of a dead sea gull lying in the wet sand along the water's edge. On the back, in German, was a short poem:

> *Deine Liebe mag sein*
> *Wie eine endlose Kette von Vögeln*
> *Zwischen Himmel und See.*
>
> *(Your love can be*
> *Like an endless chain of birds*
> *Between the heaven and the sea . . .)*

The rest of that summer my energy was endless, and I was open to and accepting everything. I had absolutely no fear. I was blissfully happy, and in some strange way people sensed it. There were gifts of flowers, poems and paintings in the house. People came to me with their troubles, and in some strange way I would be able to help. Friends told me later they'd never seen me so radiant, but I was totally unaware of it at the time. I just lived every moment.

During dinner at a friend's house, my hostess told me she and a girl friend were leaving the next day for Morocco to buy wool—they both were weavers. Straight out of the blue, I said, "May I come along?"—something I normally would never have done. But then, things weren't normal—or were they, at long last?

In high spirits, we flew to Tangiers and took a taxi to Marrakesh. Feeling ourselves much too sophisticated to be tourists, we found lodgings in the bus terminal hotel, though calling it a hotel would be to elevate it considerably. It was really a first-floor patio with rooms leading from that, plus one communal amenity which, upon first sight, produced instant constipation. The price was minimal, and worth it as long as you didn't mind sharing your room with a few other bed-

189

fellows, small in size but marching in platoons. For the next seven days, we explored and shopped and acquired objects of every kind, most of them quite unnecessary, and arrived back in Ibiza loaded down like packmules.

One day I was happily cutting and chopping and slicing and dicing, the kitchen looking as though a tornado had just passed through, when Frederik walked in the door. "what's going on?" he asked. "Not much," I answered. "I'm just having one-hundred-and-fifty people in tomorrow for a Full Moon Party. How was the trip?" At that moment, Nanny walked in and flung fourteen chickens on the table. "Oh . . . very good," he said, as Herbert Burkholz arrived with eight cases of wine. "Terry's coming to stay . . ." he added. "That's fine," as I gave him an armload of flowering thistles. "Could you please put these in water? I'll be right back to make lunch!" and I disappeared down the road.

The full moon rose and Frederik stared from an upstairs terrace in total bewilderment. There were closer to three hundred than the invited one-hundred-and-fifty. Aretha Franklin was doing her thing in our huge room downstairs, somebody else was doing his thing at the upright upstairs— I think it was "Clair de Lune," appropriately enough—and four Indian shirts were into their drums on the guest house roof. One lonely flute could be heard from somewhere in the trees. Fellini couldn't have done much better, I thought.

The following days Frederik and I talked about what had happened to me. I explained to him that, as much as he'd inflicted the illness, he'd quite unwittingly given me the cure for it, too. And not only the cure, but the inoculation against whatever might come next. It was not a case of fixing blame, but rather our both having been swept along on a predestined route.

The house was merry with loads of children, guests, song and music. Musician friends of mine came to practice because of the good acoustics and fell in love with the croaking of the frogs in the reservoir. I pride myself on having the loudest and most musical frogs on the island. It was decided they *had* to be recorded. Not only that, they were to take part in a jam

190

session. No sooner said than done: instruments and equipment were hauled down the hill and set up. The overture was struck by the trumpeter who'd crawled down the steps of the springhouse for better echo effect. After the first two notes, the frogs shut up. Everyone crouched on the edge of the pond doing his Sunday-best frog imitations, but to no avail. After two hours with the fake frogs now laryngitic and the real ones silently splitting their sides, the musicians gave up and hauled the gear back to the house. Just as they reached the door, the real frog chorus performed beautifully. And I fell off the wall laughing!

The weeks flew by. By the end of August we had to leave to organize our last engagement, a tour of South Africa. We'd held off going for years, but after listening to so many people holding forth, condemning and protesting apartheid, yet finding that almost none of them had ever been there, we decided we'd see for ourselves. The ones who blasted us the most for going when it was made public were the Dutch.

Back on the road again and under pressure, I lost some of my new-found peace of mind, and the tour seemed to drag on endlessly.A few of the bright points were the evenings and Sundays spent with Indian friends in Capetown.

South Africa is incredibly beautiful. Only by being there, however, did we realize how enormously complex the problems are. It was a bit like going back twenty years in life style. A Capetown friend of ours said, "If all of us who do not believe in the system leave, how is it ever going to change? By isolating ourselves from the rest of the world, we've kept out new ideas and progress. How can we possibly make people think and want to improve matters without outside stimulation and inspiration? Some of us have to stay to try to crack that wall of isolation."

We ended the tour in Kimberley, site of the world's biggest man-made hole in the ground—I guess everyone's got to have something to boast about! The town wasn't very large, reminiscent of the standard movie set for a Western, and neither was our theatre. In fact, the audience we faced was the smallest of the tour, but one of the very warmest. It was a terrible night, knowing it would be the last time we'd stand on stage together. Nobody knew except Frank and his wife, Rita, who were, I think, nearly as sad. We'd been together for years and had been through so much, sharing both the good times and the bad. Doing my solo medley of love songs almost finished me off, but I kept thinking of something an old actress had once said to me: *"You're* not supposed to cry, you're supposed to make the *audience* cry."

That morning, with my usual sense of amateur dramatics, I started separating our things into piles of "His" and "Hers," but we only had one large suitcase between us. I trotted down the wooden sidewalk flinching at dust and tumbleweed coming 'round the corners and feeling immensely sorry for myself. I bought the cheapest, ugliest cardboard suitcase I could find to emphasize my misery, then carted it back to the hotel and, with exaggerated neatness, packed both bags.

Frederik, an old friend and I sat in the Durban airport for a while over coffee. Then my flight was called. The mood was light—it could have been any airport and at any time. I turned back once at the top of the steps and waved, then went inside loaded down with things we'd bought—an enormous spear, two makwajans (musical instruments), a huge traveling bag full of spices from the Indian market, printed cotton materials, pottery and a large paper bag full of seashells from Inhaca, a small island we'd visited in the Indian Ocean.

I suddenly felt relieved. The parting had taken place—I no longer could see his face—and as I searched for my seat, I suddenly straightened up. It was as though I'd been lying under a mountain for an eternity, and someone had finally levered it up to let me out. There was a kind-faced American already sitting in the seat next to mine who helped me put away all my paraphernalia. As we sat down, he started chatting, asked how I had enjoyed South Africa, if I lived in London and what did I do? What *did* I do? He told me his name—what was mine now? All of a sudden, I heard myself talking of the future. Yes, I was going back to work, I was a singer. No, I was separated . . . going back to my children. Yes, three . . . Then I felt exhausted, excused myself and went to sleep.

"Nina Alone"

The children were used to our comings and goings, so I merely told them Frederik had work to do and needed quiet and solitude, so had stayed on in South Africa. I began calling long-neglected friends, I bought books and records, and the house was full of music from morning to night. So much had happened in music that I wanted to know about. My first job was for an old friend of ours, John Barry. We'd recorded with him years before, and now he was doing the sound track for the new James Bond picture, "On Her Majesty's Secret Service." My contribution was a Christmas ditty (quite in character) with a choir of deliberately off-key little, and not so little, angels. Unfortunately, they used my two minutes of music under the biggest and loudest chase scene in the film. With guns popping, cars screeching, people yelling and shouting, I was piping away to myself. My mother, who patiently sat through the movie twice, never heard a note.

I'd gone to see my mother a few weeks after my return and had told her the whole story, deliberately waiting until I had resolved the whole situation within my own mind. She cried, but was relieved to see me so at peace with myself, something she'd not seen for a long time.

My days had become busy and full of laughter, but the

193

evenings were sometimes very long. I thought I'd spend Christmas in England with just the children and close friends. Frederik and I had been writing each other throughout that fall. I scribbled away about the children and life on my own, while he wrote funny stories but very little about his domestic life and less about himself.

Christmas Day the doorbell rang and Frederik was there, very tanned and very serene. He'd never looked better. Dorothy had left Capetown with the baby. South Africa had not been the dream come true, as realized dreams rarely are, but the time spent had been necessary. However, spiritually he had found a *new* way . . . and now he wanted to spread his prayer rug here. I so loved him, but didn't know whether to laugh or cry.

I knew him so well, I felt this would be just another way-station in his search. It had lasted three months in South Africa and it would last three months here, then the restlessness would set in again. He was terribly angry and quite astounded when I told him that now he was finally free, that he should grab that freedom and enjoy it without guilt. To come back here and live in our usual sibling relationship would not satisfy him for long. We had both let go. His real longing underneath it all was to do the right thing, but knowing him, that wasn't necessarily sitting here enthroned as "Father." Free spirits can be trained but never chained (that's why I hate circuses and zoos and never go to either). After we had discussed all this, we laughed a lot and were still friends.

He left for India with his old friend Terry a couple of weeks later, and I threw myself into my dual existence of mother and performer. Trying to satisfy my own demands upon myself in either role has always produced a conflict within me. Twenty-four hours in a day just never seem enough. While doing a job, I'm totally involved in whatever's at hand, and it's only afterward that self-doubts hit me. But, I've found, if I let those doubts take over, I can do neither job, even in a mediocre fashion. So, I plow ahead, packing the most into each day, harassed but happy.

Early one Sunday in March, 1970, I was rushed to a hospital

194

with a burst appendix. That same afternoon, not feeling my brightest, I suddenly saw Frederik standing in the doorway with Terry, back from India. To use his own quote: "My timing is perfect. Whenever you can't cope, you end up in a hospital." I had my revenge for his lack of sympathy: "Quite right, and now you can go home and take over the cooking and laundry." I finally had to ask them to leave—my stitches just hurt too much from laughing. The last day of my stay I was tottering down the corridor for a bit of exercise when a young little nurse with a Scandinavian accent came up to me and shyly whispered, "You wouldn't know where I could get some grass, would you?" So much for show business people's reputation.

I swore I'd get out in a week, and I did. My fireplace in Ibiza needed rebuilding, so I decided to convalesce there. With a suitcase full of cloth for a bit of cushion-making—fifty-seven of them—plus a toothbrush, I left. My first chore was to go searching for the foreman who had restored the house years before. I knew he loved the house, and I wanted the kitchen fireplace, which had never worked, rebuilt with the old tools in the old island style. With a little help from cognac and coffee and the local songs, he and two workmen built in a week the most antique-looking, completely crooked best-drawing fireplace anyone could want. That my cushions were slightly crooked, too, was beside the point.

Back in London, I worked solidly till July, then returned to the *finca* and a lot of sailing. Frederik's catamaran was still in Ibiza, and he told me I could use it. Fearlessly, I set off, doing triple duty as skipper, first mate and cook, and learning the ropes literally by trial and error. I hadn't really sailed since my teens, so I enlisted the help of an old friend and his wife. We became the terror of the high seas and languished on several sandbars before passing fishermen took pity on us and hauled us off. I dived to chase octopus and fish and to search for missing engine parts and lost anchors, followed an enormous stingray on his early morning swim, explored caves and now and then surfaced to warm myself on the rocks. The three of us would stay away for weekends, anchoring off moonlit rocks at night and leaving anchor at sunup to catch the early morning breezes. Sometimes I'd take the children and more friends along, and at times like these the boat took on the appearance of a Chinese junk. I reaffirmed my deep love for the sea that summer.

The house was a bit like a Chinese junk, too. Friends and their children visited frequently and we usually dined at the local workmen's restaurant, "we" being anything from six to twelve or more. It was cheap, simple but well-cooked food. The rest of the time we lived off the farm. Vegetables were plentiful and in season, and the children fetched their own milk from the stables every morning at seven.

Clifford and Edith came to one of the few parties I gave that summer. (She had become his fourth wife in 1967.) I'd gone to see her the year before at their home because I wanted to tell her I felt the island was too small for old grudges. Could we not make peace between us? I didn't stay long, but it was a friendly meeting, and when she took me downstairs to the door, she asked me to dinner a few days later. I went, and it was a pleasant evening which was repeated not too long afterward. A couple of weeks later, Edith and Clifford came to my annual Full Moon Party. It looked as though we'd managed to resolve our problem.

But now, a year later at my house, Clifford had too much to drink and, with pointed remarks and unsubtle hints, undid all Edith and I had managed to establish. The evening came to an end without incident, but a day or so later, Edith appeared and asked if we could talk.

She told me she was sick of his running around, and I could have him if I wanted him. I assured her we were not seeing each other and that, furthermore, I had no intention of seeing him, adding that I was rather enjoying my newfound freedom. I was not divorced, only separated, had children and a career, I told her, and had no intention of breaking up her marriage or, for the present, my own. She seemed so upset that I finally asked her why she didn't just leave him. She answered that she couldn't walk out on him and the children unless she knew he would be happy with me. I realized then that she was trying to find a way for Clifford—and herself—to be happy. We talked for quite a while about marriage and life—no longer just about us—and concluded that men were really a bunch of rotters. On that note, we parted, and I didn't see the Irvings again that year.

By September, 1970, back in London, I was preparing my first solo cabaret act and had absolutely no idea in which direction to go musically. My inclination has always been toward the sad, melodic songs—I can get quite carried away doing those, but that's not what people want to sit and listen to for hours on end. Besides, once you've made an audience laugh, it's like an opiate and you're hooked. (However, I'm no comic.) Faithfully I went every day to my rented rehearsal studio—my Dante's Inferno, the soundproofing being nonexistent—to learn my new repertoire. The day my room was between the rooms of a trumpet and a soprano, I just gave up. My pianist, Sid, bless his soul, would accompany me with endless patience. I had completely lost my first surge of enthusiasm for a career, to say nothing of my self-confidence, when I met John Marshall and his wife, Elizabeth, at a cocktail party. John had been producing and managing in show business since early youth, and we started discussing my work. He had recently been managing another artist and was now looking around for a replacement. When I told him I'd decided to give up my career to move to Ibiza, he immediately set out to dissuade me, suggesting that we meet again and have another chat. I subsequently went down to his country home where Liz, as she's known among friends, served a delicious lunch. In a strange way, she reminded me of myself ten years earlier, and we look so much alike we're very often taken for sisters.

John wanted to hear what I was preparing for my cabaret act and came to rehearsal a few days later. We decided to work together. He saw a challenge in establishing me as a solo artist, and I badly needed his enthusiasm, encouragement and faith in my abilities. After being half of a successful duo, I knew it would be more difficult to establish myself in my own career than if starting from scratch. I'd heard it said so many times, "Oh, yes, she's very good, but what a pity they split up . . ."

I'd always been the immovable object (Frederik and I used the same stand mike) and had never spoken to the audience (he did all the talking). Suddenly, there I was on the stage of the "Golden Garter" in Manchester, floundering around like a lost goldfish, clutching a handmike and tripping over the train of my dress in my eagerness to prove I could move. What it really proved was that I hadn't lost the two left feet of my college days, both of them hopelessly entangled in the cord of the mike. Full marks to the audience and John for patience.

The "Golden Garter" holds about eight hundred persons if I remember correctly. The booze is free-flowing and it can get quite noisy at times, but the audience was very receptive and quiet. The few remarks that did come across the footlights were only funny and actually flattering. I survived it all and returned to London to change the act, under John's tutoring, as much as time allowed before opening at the Savoy three weeks later.

That opening night I was paralyzed with fear. I'd stood on that stage with Frederik and knew the audience well, and I felt if I could just turn around, he'd still be there. Oddly enough, I discovered my greatest fear was of forgetting lyrics, a thing I'd done only once in all the years I'd worked with Frederik. The Golden Rule is: Don't stop no matter what happens—just keep going! And I did, learning the art of instant poetry at the same time. There were nights when Frank Sinatra would never have recognized "My Way . . ." John was there every night with pep talks and advice and I became more confident.

During the next year, I did cabarets in Stockholm, Copenhagen, and guested on television shows in England and other parts of Europe. I also did an extraordinary outdoor show in Oslo on a gypsy caravan in the middle of a race course at midnight! I can't remember what the purpose of my being there really was—it was some kind of festival and, although summer, it was so terribly cold the musicians were on stage in overcoats and woolen scarfs. I gave up changing, and sat on the edge of the stage in my sweater and boots and chatted and sang.

Under John Marshall's management there was now a lot of

198

work and little time for private life other than being with the children. My mother came to London and babysat the times I was abroad for more than a week. I'm very lucky in that respect: she loves London, spoils the kids rotten and they take full advantage of it.

Christmas, 1970, the children and I went to visit my parents-in-law in Holland where they had now moved. For the first time, Clara, Frederik's sister, and her children and our children spent Christmas together. With seven children the same ages it was quite a houseful and as the days wore on the mothers wore down. It was a real country Christmas with snow and horses and sleighs. Too soon we had to leave.

Sometime in January, Clifford called from Ibiza and said he'd be coming through London en route to New York and would like to say hello. He arrived in early February and spent the afternoon chatting in my kitchen—it was good to see him again. At dinner that evening, we brought each other up to date on our doings. I told him with excitement how well things were going for me. He told me about his marriage, which was limping along, about his suspecting Edith's having found a German boy friend and their having discussed divorce. He still wanted to marry me, but I looked him straight in the eye and laughingly asked if we hadn't both had enough of that.

The next day at lunch, Clifford asked me if I had a few days free to go to the Bahamas with him. I rarely do things on the spur of the moment, but I suddenly heard myself say "Yes." I cleared my working schedule with John, and it was all right —I did need a vacation, and it'd be for only four days. His last words to me were, "Have fun, but for God's sake, be discreet!"

I joined Clifford in New York a few days later, and he asked me if I'd like to go to Mexico instead. He knew a small town south of Mexico City where he'd spent some time and wanted to show it to me, and I'd never been to Mexico, anyway, so —why not?

We took off for Mexico the next day, changed planes in New Orleans and arrived late Thursday afternoon in Mexico

City, both very tired from the trip. It was during the drive from the airport to our hotel that Clifford suddenly turned to me and said in a low voice that he was going to write the autobiography of Howard Hughes, that it was a great secret and he couldn't reveal any more. He added that he might possibly have to meet Hughes while we were there, but I was not to talk about this project. Nothing more was mentioned and we chatted happily about the sights gliding by outside and whether we'd go out on the town that night. Howard Hughes to me was an American millionaire who dabbled in the movies. I knew nothing of him or his eccentricities—if Clifford had mentioned Getty or Onassis or Rockefeller, that would have been different!

Clifford checked us in at the Reina Maria Christina. We finally got a room facing the courtyard and away from the noises of the street. By this time, any thoughts we'd entertained earlier of going out on the town had vanished in our fatigue. Around 1:00 A.M., we awakened and ordered whatever we could from room service at that hour. The town was undoubtedly asleep by then, so we decided to do likewise before catching the plane to Oaxaca at dawn.

Next morning the weather was clear and we took off in a doubtful-looking twin-prop plane, hoping it would hold together until we reached our destination. By noon we had made it and took a taxi to the Hotel Victoria, a small modern hotel on a hillside overlooking the town and its environs. Clifford got us a bungalow, part of a compound belonging to the hotel and with a communal swimming pool (not one of my favorite things). There were trees and flowers all around, and complete peace.

Our days in Oaxaca were wonderful. We were comfortable with each other—there were no pretenses and there were no tensions. Somehow the whole thing was like the running joke we had between us: we'd always said that one day we'd meet in an old-age pensioners' home and sit next to each other in rocking chairs—wheelchairs, even—unable to move and just talk and talk and talk. Clifford did so like to talk!

Clifford asked if I wanted to go to the beach, knowing my

love for the sea and dislike for pools, so Sunday morning we loaded our rented Volkswagon with food and wine—crazy, perhaps, as it was nearly two hundred miles to the Pacific Coast, but the day was beautiful, the scenery magnificent and we had nothing else to do. On the lonely rockstrewn beach, we alternated between sips of wine in the warm Mexican sun and plunges into the icy sea to clear our heads. We returned to the Victoria quite late, showered and changed and went down to dinner, dancing and several Margaritas. We chatted about his travels, about Ibiza gossip and his unfinished novel, the first chapter of which I'd read and liked, and he spoke again of Hughes.

"I'm not really meeting Hughes, you know," he said, "but I am writing his autobiography." He said "autobiography," but he could also have said "biography"—it didn't matter then, for I didn't know the difference (I know now!). I must have looked puzzled, because I remember his saying, "Oh, I'm writing it as if he were telling the story." After that we talked of other things.

As in Ibiza, there was a curfew in this never-never-land, too. The four days were glorious, but we both had to get back to the responsibilities of our real lives: he to Ibiza and his work, I to London to prepare for a concert a few weeks later at Festival Hall. He was in London to see his publishers the day of my concert, so he attended, then joined a group of us for supper at the Dorchester. There we said goodnight, and he was off the next day.

Occasionally, Clifford would call me from Ibiza to say hello and ask what I was doing. We were very attached to each other at that time, and after those calls I'd think about our seeing each other again and wonder: was that attachment really a way of holding on to something that once was?

John arranged a contract with Pye Records that spring for my first solo LP, not inappropriately titled, "Nina Alone." I don't really like recording very much; I need the warmth and reaction of an audience. It's so cold and impersonal to stand between soundproof movable boards with earphones on, knowing that somebody in another room can make you sound like Tiny Tim or Tweetie Pie just by twiddling knobs and pushing buttons. This time I was working with a large orchestra and strings. Having been used to a small group for so many years, I had to make sure I didn't become so pre-occupied with the orchestra's rich sound that I forgot to sing. The only way this album registered with my five-year-old daughter came out as we were riding in a cab a short while later.

"Say, aren't you Nina of 'Nina and Frederik?' " asked the driver.

Ana Maria bounced up in her seat and retorted: "No, she isn't . . . she's Nina Alone!"

And Kirsa chimed in, "Daddy's off doing his own thing!"

I went to Ibiza in late May to do a photographic session with John for the jacket of the record, and to see how the workmen were getting on with the repairs. Having no telephone, I couldn't alert Eulalia and arrived exhausted on the midnight flight, wondering how on earth I was going to get into my house unless the key was in its usual place. I took a taxi to La Tierra Bar and, having greeted Arlene, the much-loved queen and mother-confessor, psychiatrist and logbook for the entire island, I turned round to find Clifford by himself at the table behind me. Edith was away in Germany. He offered me a ride home and, luckily, the key was there. We talked for a short while in the cold musty living room over a glass of sour wine, arranging to meet at the beach the next day, and then he took off.

We picnicked at Figuerales the following afternoon. The day was warm and as the beach was deserted, I took my top off and was wading among the rocks collecting stones when I looked up and saw Clifford with his camera. My first reaction was concern, but knowing him so well, I felt I had no need to worry. (Little did I know that Edith, after finding the pictures in his studio, would later give them to a member of the press on the condition that he get them well publicized. However, bearing no malice, he contacted me instead and returned the pictures.)

John arrived that night but had forgotten his camera, so the next two days were a round-the-clock rush of finding and borrowing another, getting the pictures done, and then off to London again.

In June, Clifford had passed through London while I was in Ibiza. Upon my return, my housekeeper asked if it were all right that she'd put him up for the night. Unbeknownst to me, he'd phoned her and asked if he could stay there, a not uncommon thing for my many friends to do.

I spent the first three weeks of July rehearsing and taping a TV special, preparing a pilot for a series which never materialized, organizing the children for their yearly dancing matinee and getting everybody's summer clothes in order. Nicolas and Kirsa left first to stay with the family in Holland and on the twenty-fourth, Ana Maria and I flew to Majorca, where I was booked for eight days. When my engagement had ended the children flew in from Amsterdam, and we all went on to Ibiza. I found the island buzzing with gossip and excitement. There had been clashes and street fights between the Spaniards and groups of hippies now living in communes in the hills near Santa Eulalia. I still don't know where fact leaves off and fiction begins, but this was another manifestation of the major change and dissension between the locals and the foreigners.

"Hippies" is a term I don't like—I'm not even sure what it means: does it describe a mode of dress or a style of living? If it means a search for simplicity, then "hippies" have been around since time immemorial. The tragedy is that anyone in blue jeans, long hair and beads is synonymous with "dropout" and drugs. Until a few years ago, we were all simply dressed and often shoeless, but it took only a small group of *real* dropouts who shoplifted, stole from the farmers, broke the honor system of credit in the shops and violated the unwritten code of behavior and traditions of the island to ruin it for everyone and forever slam the door shut on Paradise.

One effort of conciliation was made by the priest in San Carlos, the village nearest the groups of communes. He arranged a folk concert one afternoon in his church—unheard of on Ibiza—and introduced it with the following words: "God's house should be a place where everyone can meet, and music the bridge that crosses all barriers. I now entrust you with God's house and only ask you not to applaud." The church was filled with foreigners, all very young, all very long-haired, in their "hippie" gear. Children were running around, babies were being nursed, as a young Canadian sat before the altar with his guitar and began to sing. An incredible peace and harmony settled over the congregation, and now and then we'd all join in the singing. After an hour-and-a-half, we filed out silently.

During my three weeks on the island, I heard from several friends that Clifford had told them "in sworn secrecy" that he was doing a book on Hughes, meeting him in out-of-the-way corners of the world, and that there were huge sums of money involved, since he was already an established writer with McGraw-Hill. Soon, half the island *knew* he was into a hush-hush thing, but you just weren't supposed to *talk* about it . . . very much in character with Clifford's love for intrigue and secrecy.

Then it was on to Poland where Nancy Wilson and I were both special guests at a summer song festival. And so it went: Oslo, Amsterdam, London, Bristol, back to London—my professional calendar was well filled.

In October I had a phone call telling me that our catamaran was lying on the bottom of the Mediterranean, and I had to fly down. Luckily, I had five days off. I'd lent the boat to some friends who had taken beautiful care of it, even to the point of pitching a tent on a cliff above the cove where it was anchored to keep an eye on it. A freak storm, the likes of which they'd not seen for fifty years, blew up, lifting the boat —anchor, cement block and all—straight onto the rocks. What was left was a skeleton, hardly worth salvaging. The friends who'd borrowed the boat were terribly upset, especially the one who'd tented out to watch it. I told him of having just left another friend who was grieving over his six-year-old daughter who had leukemia and only a few months to live. How, then, could anyone get hysterical over the loss of a half-ton of plywood?

After I'd filed the claim papers, I drove into town to Clifford's studio to ask him about the pictures from the beach, which bothered me. He was there with Richard Suskind, knee-deep in piles of manuscript, file folders, yellow pads and stacks of loose papers. I'd known Suskind casually for some time—he'd been a frequent visitor to Ibiza—and Clifford had told me he was handling a good deal of the research for the Hughes book. After Suskind had gone, we searched for the photos but Clifford had hidden them so well, we couldn't find them. He promised to look later and send them to me, then he and I sat over a bottle of wine and talked, rambling through my life in London, my work and the gossip on Ibiza.

As we were reminiscing, he suddenly pulled out a drawer in his gray filing cabinet and proceeded to read things I'd said at our first meetings seven years before! Hearing them again gave me a queer feeling, and then I saw he'd typewritten on index cards the mots and philosophical nuggets of almost everyone else he knew—to be used in his work! I told him I felt as though I were being rolled on silent rollers into the past, into his "Morgue of Thoughts and Souls."

Finally, he began talking quite animatedly about the Hughes project, and showed me the letters Hughes had written to him. He had a good deal of manuscript and asked if I'd like to read some of it. I leafed through several sections, but the only anecdote I recall had something to do with shoplifting a bag of cookies. However, even this episode was so filled with unknown names and references that it made very little sense to me. My curiosity would have been greater about another book he'd worked on—the true-life stories of four foreigners on Ibiza—but they chickened out and he shelved it. He pointed toward the stacks of typescript and said they were all the transcriptions of his taped interviews with Hughes. One stack of pages, separate from the rest, was a manuscript he'd obtained from another writer. There was, he assured me, "some really marvelous stuff" in it.

Then he asked if I would like to hear one of the taped interviews, but I said I hadn't time. He laughed heartily and said to forget it, since he and Suskind had actually interviewed each other, and I went flying out the door.

205

The next day when I saw him to say goodbye, I told him of the trip John and I would be making in November to California and Las Vegas regarding work. He said he thought he might be in the States at that time and would try to see me then.

John and I left for America November 7, 1971, stopping first in New York to see all the cabaret shows we could possibly squeeze into our schedule. It was always interesting for me to see how other acts worked, and in this case especially, since he was planning to start me in America the following year. We went on to Dallas, my first visit there, and experienced the famous Texas hospitality I'd heard about, then on to Los Angeles ending up in Vegas on the nineteenth. We stayed there for four days. The only way I can describe Vegas is "one has to see it to believe it." To my astonishment, the operator answering the phone every morning began by saying, "Good evening." I know that the Chinese and Jews don't use our calendar, and maybe they didn't believe in Greenwich Mean Time, but this was absurd! Both I and my sinuses are adverse to air conditioning, and when I spied with my bloodshot eyes the greenery fifteen stories below, I quickly grabbed a book, went downstairs and wended my way through a maze of corridors out to the pool. It was the closest thing I'd seen to a perfect lawn since leaving England, but as I set foot on it, the first squeak was unmistakably plastic. Astroturf, they call it—well, the Astros can have it, whoever they are! While staying at the International, John arranged for me to work there the coming spring. I looked forward to this, having met everyone connected with the hotel. They'd all gone out of their way to make our stay enjoyable. To me, it was unbelieveable to see so many famous names of show business in one place, and we spent our evenings rushing from one show to another. Since I don't gamble, I used to go for long walks and usually found myself the only soul on the sidewalk—doesn't anyone *walk* in Vegas?

After four hectic days, we returned to L. A. where Clifford joined us the following evening, Thanksgiving Eve. We were staying in a house in Beverly Hills loaned to us by friends.

206

Clifford brought the now completed manuscript with him and some drawings of Hughes that he'd commissioned from David Walsh, explaining that Hughes did not want his picture taken and would accept only an artist's interpretation. While I cooked dinner, he and John talked. Clifford's anecdotes were endless, especially about the elaborate rituals he'd undergone at the times of his meetings with Hughes.

The next day, Clifford suggested that we drive up the coast over the weekend to Big Sur and Monterey where he had once lived. At that moment, John walked in. I told him of Clifford's suggestion and asked if we had any appointments for the next two days. There were none, he thought it'd be a good idea for us to go, and left. Then Clifford dug into me, saying it was absurd I couldn't come and go as I wanted, asking why on earth I was working so hard—was I really that ambitious? It was all very well for him to talk, I replied annoyedly, but who was going to educate my children the way I wanted, sort out the bills, et cetera, et cetera. Of course, I added, I was tired, too, at times, but in Frederik's and my mercurial business (and especially in view of our separation), whoever was earning money at the moment paid the bills.

Late Friday afternoon, we set out on the inland route for Monterey, and stopped for dinner and the night halfway. Saturday, we drove on to Big Sur, where Clifford become very reminiscent, telling me of his life in California during the 50's and about his second wife Claire's tragic death there. We spent most of the day in the Monterey and Carmel areas, where we went to the local cinema that evening. Arriving back at our hotel too late for dinner, we decided to have a couple of Margaritas for old time's sake. The talk both in the bar and back in our room was of ideals, goals and our children, and then commitments, but there was hardly any common ground. It was almost as though he had no commitments at all—was there no inner life?

He went on about the farm he'd just bought in Ibiza and his plans for redoing it once he'd wrapped up the Hughes project. Clifford anticipated some flak when the book was announced and speculated then that Hughes, unpredictable as he was,

207

would undoubtedly denounce the whole thing. He also wanted to get back to his long novel and just find peace and quiet after the hectic year he'd just spent.

He suddenly asked if I'd like to see a lot of money. Without waiting for an answer, he pulled out a check made out to "H. R. Hughes" and signed by the president of McGraw-Hill. The amount was astronomical—$250,000., as I recall.

"That's what I'm supposed to give to Hughes," he said holding it up. I don't remember what his next words were, for I suddenly knew something was desperately wrong. I went cold.

"I don't want to hear anymore about it," I said. "Whatever you're up to, if you're up to anything, don't do it!" I went to bed and didn't talk to him anymore—I just tuned out.

At seven the next morning, I woke him and told him I wanted to leave. We hardly spoke to each other en route back to Los Angeles, arriving at the house well before lunch. While John and Clifford watched a football game on television, I began cleaning up and preparing the house for our departure.

Clifford left for New York the following day, and I left for London Tuesday, changing planes in New York. I had coffee with him there—a short and strained interlude—then he was off to McGraw-Hill and I to buy presents for the children.

I worked in London all through December into New Year's, 1972, and Frederik joined the children and me for Christmas. Whenever he was in town, he'd always come to see the children and I'd cook him a good dinner—or sometimes it was the other way round if I were working. I would discuss my work with him, and he seemed very pleased that things were going so well. He'd been working on a film script in Rome, but as so often happened in that industry, the project fell through. He was still writing songs on and off but only for his own pleasure.

In January, Clifford phoned me from New York. I was already late for a rehearsal and wouldn't have taken the call had it not been from America. "Everything's gone crazy," he said.

"What're you talking about?," I asked.

He said he'd be coming through London en route to Ibiza in a week and would tell me then. I told him I was supposed to go to Copenhagen, but in truth I really didn't want to see him. That was the last time I talked with him.

New York

At the end of January, I was invited with John and Liz Marshall to visit some friends in the Bahamas. I was so looking forward to a week in the sun with nothing to do, and the first three days were glorious. The fourth morning, someone came down to our beach bungalow and said a gentleman from the U.S. Postal Department in Washington wanted to see me. A few minutes later, a soft-spoken gentleman with a briefcase walked in, introduced himself as Mr. Brady and said, "I'd like to speak to you about Clifford Irving. I must advise you I have already contacted the island authorities in case you're not prepared to answer my questions." He said that he knew I'd been in Mexico with Clifford and just wanted to verify a few things, things he obviously already knew about. Would I mind telling him in my own words about the trip? Of course not. The only time he interrupted me was when I forgot the short layover in New Orleans on the flight from New York to Mexico City. Only when I'd finished did I see that he already had on his clipboard flight numbers, names of hotels, time schedules, in fact the whole thing.

John Marshall was with me throughout the entire interview, at the end of which Mr. Brady asked if he knew Clifford, too.

John told him of Clifford's visit with us the preceding November in Beverly Hills, describing documents, papers and pictures Clifford had shown him them. Mr. Brady thanked us and asked if we would be prepared to go to New York and repeat in front of the Federal Grand Jury what we had told him. We both agreed and asked him to join us for lunch. John picked up a London paper en route to the restaurant. The headline was:

FBI SEEKS DANISH SINGER IN
CONNECTION WITH HUGHES HOAX

I just sat there and stared at that newspaper, as if I were reading about somebody else. It was dated February 2; my mother-in-law's birthday was the next day, and this would be in her morning paper. I felt sick. Suddenly, the sun was not warm anymore. My immediate reaction was concern for my children and family and whomever else this headline might upset. To be at the mercy of the particularly sensational papers would be hell for all concerned. The ironic thing was that the FBI wasn't looking for me at all. It was the Postal Department as represented by Mr. Brady, but I suppose "Postal Department" doesn't sound so dramatic as "FBI" in a banner headline.

John took charge right away. After lunch he sent Liz and me off to the beach while he went to the hotel to make plane reservations for London. That afternoon, the phones started ringing from all parts of the world. The first interview was with John Goldmann of *The Los Angeles Times* who, after talking with John and me, read us part of Clifford's affidavit about meeting Hughes in Mexico, the first time we'd heard of that or any affidavit. Shortly after, Morris Nessen, Clifford's lawyer in New York, phoned and John took the call. Nessen said he had a message from Irving: tell Nina Clifford loves her, and not to talk to the authorities.

John told him it was too late: the authorities had already been there that morning and had known beforehand the details of the Mexico trip. Nessen said they'd missed us by a few hours—they'd had detectives out looking for me for two days.

211

After talking it over, John thought the best course of action was for him to go back, call my mother and family and see the press while we stayed on. But he soon changed his mind. A Canadian connected with the hotel had already taken off Wednesday afternoon for Miami, where he tipped off the press as to my whereabouts and then offered "his own story," whatever that might have been. The next morning Liz and I were on the beach when a cameraman suddenly leaped at us from the bushes. We fled to the house. John decided we'd all better leave, and we started packing. A knock came—it was a TV crew from CBS. They agreed to wait while we finished packing, then drove us in to the airport where we gave them an interview.

It was through this crew and the other journalists now pouring in through the tiny airport that we kept abreast of the latest news from New York. Only then did it begin to dawn on us how dramatic a development my statement had been. I just wanted to go home. It was as if, in some kind of insanity, I believed all this would disappear within the safety of my own home. John and Liz were wonderful. We went straight back to London, and even though John had prepared me for the scene at Heathrow Airport, it was a hideous nightmare. The barrage of questions from the hundreds of newsmen, cameramen, photographers was like running the gauntlet. John never left my side and fended off all questions.

To help me avoid the press and have some privacy, John invited me to stay with them, and Liz fetched the children. I wanted them with me and away from all the turmoil. John called Frederik. I didn't dare—I was terrified of what his reaction would be. In my depression, I was imagining the worst: would he take the children from me? In Switzerland, where we'd been married and were domiciled, the law, always favoring the man, would be on his side if he decided to do so.

He came down the same afternoon and, to my immense relief, laughed: "You're the only one I know who could wade with great big duck feet completely blindfolded into a situation like this!" He then provided us with the first laugh we'd had since the news had broken: "I've got the title for your next single—'Knock, Knock, Hughes There?' "

Frederik had brought my mail and a list of phone messages. There were several from Clifford. Later, Mary, my housekeeper, told me he'd asked her for my address, saying it was most urgent that he find me. But she'd always had standing instructions never to let anyone except the immediate family know of my whereabouts, and she hadn't budged.

John dealt with all the press, the ones who phoned at all hours of night and day, the others who even drove down to the house.

I refused to read the papers, trying to isolate myself from the outside world and pretend it didn't exist. I was with the children and, happily, they knew nothing of what was going on and were enjoying their stay in the country. But, how would it be for us to live with the shadow of this publicity following us for the rest of our lives? The thought of what it was doing to my mother tortured me.

A few days later while Don Short of the *London Daily Mirror* was at the house, John phoned Nessen in New York. By coincidence, Clifford was in Nessen's offices. John told them we were sorry for what had happened, but that we had had no option but to answer Brady's questions. It had been heavily implied in the Scandinavian press that I was an accomplice and very much part of the whole plot (my mother had crank phone calls for months afterward). I heard part of the conversation but left, and just couldn't listen later to the tape John had made.

I'd thought the difficult times had ended, at least for a while, and there would be time to rest. I was deeply depressed, and even though John and Liz, and Frederik, too, did their best to cheer me up, inside I felt sick.

On Thursday, February 10, John, Liz and I left for New York, as John and I were scheduled to appear before the grand jury the next day. An American friend of my mother's had given me the name of her attorney, Richard Russell, who would meet us at the airport. John cautioned me on the plane about the reputed aggressiveness of the American press and told me to answer all questions with "No comment," two words I got to know almost better than my own name in the next few days.

The throng of press at Kennedy Airport and later at the St. Regis, where we stayed, was unbelievable. The American journalists I had feared turned out to be good-humored and polite, though at times a little eager, and were all very kind. One thing that amused me was the way they would shout, "Hey, Brrrrrness!," at least that's what it sounded like to me. When shown to our rooms, we were told we could call the house detectives if necessary—I found that odd at the time. But then came the nasty threatening phone calls. The anonymous ones were bad enough, but the messages from the "friends" from Ibiza were the worst, telling me I was "putting Irving behind bars," was a "stool pigeon," and so they went on.

Richard Russell told us our appointments with both the Federal and State Grand Juries had been postponed until Monday. With the pressure that surrounded us, Monday seemed an eternity away.

Over the weekend, I resolved to repeat to the Grand Jury exactly what I had told Mr. Brady, no more, no less. Although evidence against Clifford was rapidly building up from all sides, to know that it was I who had unwittingly given the investigators their first break was devastating.

My first reaction after talking with Brady had been disbelief. How had Clifford and I, two private beings wanting to be together, suddenly become major characters in an international scandal? Our relationship had been dragged down to gutter level and was now bandied about over every bar, in every office, in millions of American homes and seemingly everywhere else. Then, when I heard of the the affidavit, describing his trip to Mexico and his meeting with Hughes, I realized I'd been used! It didn't anger me—it just hurt. How could he who had professed to love me implicate me in this horror? My thoughts always came back to that . . . and I had loved him, too. What could he possibly expect me to do? The Grand Jury hearings—the Federal was first, then the State— didn't take very long. After recounting what I had told Mr. Brady, I was asked if Clifford had ever indicated to me that the book was a hoax. I answered, "No." I knew I should have

214

said "Yes," but I just couldn't do it. Afterward, I somehow stopped my mind from thinking about the possible consequences of my lie, but I didn't sleep for two nights.

I'd just shut myself in my room and stare . . . couldn't concentrate on anything. I'd go for walks very early when no one was around . . . bundle myself up so no one would recognize me. Then I was alone, which I wanted, or rather, in the *aloneness* that I wanted. It was such a relief, and I clung to it for a short while, believing that nothing was really going on. It was only a postponement of my thoughts and I became fascinated with small details of life in the street, things you ordinarily never see but which are so much a part of "now." You experience life as one quick flash after another of "now," for the future is unbearable to think of—and to think of the past is useless. I really didn't even think of the future, for there wasn't one as far as I was concerned.

Then Richard Russell phoned me at eight in the morning. I was out walking, but when I got his message, I knew immediately why he had called. I walked into his office and, before he could say anything, said, "Yes. I lied and I know what you're going to say." He arranged that morning for me to return to the Grand Jury.

They repeated their questions on my meeting with Mr. Brady, then again asked if Clifford had ever indicated to me that the book was a hoax. I told them what he'd said in Mexico and about my visits to his studio in Ibiza, about the manuscripts and the tape, and the check he'd shown me in California, and explained my reactions at those instances. I think they understood. I then apologized and was excused.

I'd been numb and almost mechanical since that first day in the Bahamas and now, sitting on the plane for home that Sunday, felt totally drained. Those nine days in New York had seemed like a lifetime. Seeing my children when I walked in the door was like coming back to life. They knew I was coming home and were waiting up for me. There were flowers everywhere, the candles were lit, and it was warm and cozy. Immediately we opened presents, checked out "Rabbit's" new clothes, how blackbirds make nests, and Nicolas's latest car-

215

toon series, "The Non-Existent Bugs." Mary brought coffee from my own coffee pot and the gingerbread cookies the children had made. We set up the "whiz cars" in the living room and, though it was late, we all sat on the floor and played Monopoly.

Epilogue

NEW YORK, APRIL 4, 1972 . . . and the opening at the St. Regis was over, the reviews had come out and were good.

In the twenty-four hours, our staid three-room suite turned into bedlam. John was in his element: visitors crowding in, the three phones ringing nonstop, more interviews, more television and radio, offers of all kinds, including product endorsements (some-funny, some ridiculous), *Playboy, Vogue, Harper's Bazaar,* and then talk of films.

While John and Lois slaved away—John was indefatigable —Liz and I slipped away in the morning to shop and get a bit of exercise, at first with the children and later on our own. The pace of New York was so different from London. People hurried along as if wound up like little dolls in high gear, and we felt almost guilty window shopping at our leisurely pace.

At the end of the first week, my mother and the children left. I hadn't spent as much time with them as I would have liked and I think my mother was exhausted. The children had had a marvelous time. With F.A.O. Schwartz right around the corner, the hansom cabs just a block farther, free mints from the lady in the hotel's newsstand and the Sabrett hot dog carts on every corner, it had been paradise! Usually, they'd both crawl into my bed at seven in the morning, turn on the television and we'd all watch "Yogi Bear" and "The Roadrunner," me with my eyes closed. The night before they left, they came to the first show, and I could hear Kirsa singing along with most of the songs.

The Maisonette was a lovely room to work in. As I waited backstage, the waiters would rush by with the last drinks and dinners before the show started, whispering to me, "It's a nice crowd tonight," wish me luck and disappear through the red velvet curtain. John watched every show with a hawk's eye to be certain nothing went wrong, turning only to chide a rare noisy guest with a friendly remark, and Walt and the band did a incredible job.

After the second show, John, Liz and I would have supper upstairs, usually joined by Walt and Jack and sometimes Derek, and rehash the night's performances before the stream of visitors arrived. Wine would be served to everyone, the conversation flowing till the early hours of the morning. Friends emerged from the past and from all corners of the world, and we made lots of new friends, too.

It was usually four or five in the morning before the last guest left. Half asleep, but ever mindful of our mothers' teachings (old habits never die), Liz Marshall and I would empty ashtrays, fluff up pillows, collect the glasses and cups and wheel the room service cart out into the corridor. Standing there, with the flaps of the white tablecloth folded up over the huge pile of debris, it looked almost macabre. With our late-night sick sense of humor, we'd sometimes plant a slightly faded flower on its "chest."

Robert Altman, the film director, came to see us and said he'd seen me on the "Carson Show" and wanted me for a part in his next film, "The Long Goodbye." It was adapted from Raymond Chandler's mystery novel and would star Elliott Gould. Although Bob Altman was sure of his choice, United Artists insisted upon a screen test. John knew how desperately I wanted to do the film and arranged for us to go to Hollywood as soon as I'd finished in New York.

Frederik came over during the last week and took me to the

Russian Tea Room to give me a proper send-off for my screen test: champagne, caviar and blinis. He told me of his plans for improving the farm in Ibiza, and I signed over the house to him. My deep attachment to it and the island was still there, but one has to learn how to let go and, in view of what had happened, Ibiza was a closed chapter.

After the final show, Frank Banks sent up champagne and a buffet, and he and his wife joined all of us who had been part of the show, both on stage and behind the scenes, plus whoever else came along that night.

One always reaches the last night with mixed emotions. An engagement of any duration is always an intense experience, unlike the hundreds of daily busy-nesses of all our lives, and becomes such a definite commitment to memory. One is tired, very tired, and glad it's over with. Yet, to say goodbye to the people with whom one's shared the experience, especially if it's been as unusual and beautiful as the St. Regis had been for us, is particularly painful. There were laughter and tears and loving words and promises to meet again. And for the last time, now alone, as Liz had already gone on to England, I emptied the ashtrays, fluffed the pillows, opened the windows and rolled "the last farewell" outside.

John and I spent five days in Hollywood as guests at Robert Altman's Malibu home. The test was done in one day, with Elliott Gould playing his own role in the movie, that of Philip Marlowe, the detective, and I playing Eileen Wade, the part for which I was being considered. Everyone was most helpful, the atmosphere very relaxed and informal, and I was so tired I could only enjoy the experience and not worry about the outcome. Bob, however, was happy with the test and introduced me to Dan Blocker, who was to play my husband. (His sudden, tragic death a short time afterward almost shelved the picture. Luckily, Bob managed to sign Sterling Hayden instead for the part.) John and I flew that Friday to Puerto Rico for a two-week engagement at the Caribe Hilton—and a week later, we heard from Hollywood that I would be in the film.

We arrived in San Juan to find my picture plastered all over the hotel advertising "The Singing Baroness in the Hughes

219

Affair." I had to count to ten to stop myself from screaming in rage and humiliation, and John was furious. To cool off, I went to my room, turned on the air conditioning full blast till my goose pimples almost popped, then sat down and started to sneeze, leaving John to sort things out downstairs. The public relations lady who was responsible never surfaced again during my stay. Walt Levinski and his wife were with us and, although we enjoyed the sea, the sand and the palm trees, I had only one thing in mind: to get home. After two weeks, I boarded that long-dreamed-of plane. There had to be a detour through New York to tie up some loose ends, have a happy reunion at the St. Regis, do some last interviews—and return to Foley Square. I had been asked by the Federal probation officer handling Clifford and Edith Irving's case to go down there to give a character reference, one of the many he'd consider in recommending the duration of their sentences, and I was glad to do so. I had nothing negative whatsoever to say about either Clifford or Edith, which he duly noted.

The plane for London was at 10:00 P.M., just enough time to pull on my blue jeans. Linda Myers, publicity director of Walker Publishing and with whom I had by now spent a lot of time discussing my book, and Walt Levinski bundled me, sixty pounds of sheet music and whatever into a cab for the airport. By the time we reached JFK, we were starved, and no restaurant facilities were open—we couldn't even buy a candy bar.

In the waiting room, two elderly, very generously endowed ladies were sitting across from us with what, to us in our ravenous state, looked like an enormous picnic basket of goodies. We died a little with their every crunch of peanuts, popcorn and chocolate candies, desperately plotting how we could either lure them away from the picnic basket or lure the basket away from them. We got to the point where we were ready to salvage the candy bar wrappers from the rubbish bin and lick them! I laughed so hard, my false eyelashes (I was still in stage makeup from "The Dick Cavett Show" I'd taped just before leaving) started coming unstuck—it was like looking at the world through a hairbrush. I eventually boarded and, to

220

lessen the hunger cramps and stifle the growling, pulled the safety belt as tight as it would go. But, by the time dinner was served, I was sound asleep. I knew I was going home, and that was all that mattered.